Contents

Acknowledgements

Introduction and scope of this review vii

Executive summary ix

1 Definitions of community mediation 1
Definitions of community mediation 1
Definition by inclusion 1
Definition by exclusion 3
Community mediation and neighbour mediation within this review 3
Conciliation vs. mediation 4
Mapping of other forms of mediation 5

2 Service providers 14
Models of provision 14
The future of local authority managed services 16
Paid and volunteer mediators 17

3 Service provision 20
Mediation UK's service membership 20
An analysis of traditional neighbour mediation cases 22
What type of mediation is used? 27
Shuttle mediation – a contradiction of usage 29
Pre-mediation activities – the development of assessment services 31
Other forms of neighbourhood-based mediation 33

4 Service users 38
Take-up of mediation by black and minority ethnic communities 38
Monitoring other than by ethnicity 40
Involving children in mediation 42
Specific service comments on involving children 42

5 Service funders 44
Details of funding sources and levels 44
Private income for mediation services 47
Service sustainability 50
Local authority support and funding 52
Mediation services and the dilemma of social landlord funding 53
The impact of Best Value 55
Does mediation work? The cost-effectiveness of mediation 56
National government funding – England 59
National government funding – Scotland and Wales 60

6 Quality standards 63
A brief history of mediation standard-setting 63
Quality systems 64
Quality systems and the community mediation field 65
Accreditation of services 66
Accreditation of mediators 68
Accreditation of training courses 70
Summary of accreditation and QM standards 71

7 Future trends and tensions | 74
Service sustainability and capacity-building | 74
Engagement in violent conflict | 75
Mediation UK and victim–offender mediation | 75
The impact of the Quality Mark | 76
Payment of mediators | 76
Academic criticism | 76

Bibliography | 79

Appendix: Methodology | 81

Acknowledgements

The following community mediation services and organisations gave their time for individual telephone interviews: Bolton, Bridge Builders, Bristol, Cardiff, Dacorum, Edinburgh, The Environment Council, Fife, Kirklees, Leeds, Luton, Manchester, National Council for Voluntary Organisations, Newham Conflict and Change Project, Wolverhampton.

We also spoke individually to:
- Ken Allcock, South Worcestershire Mediation
- Annie Beardsley, Bath Area Mediation
- Tony Billinghurst, Director, Mediation UK
- Heather Bradbury, Head of ADR Unit, Lord Chancellor's Department
- Diane English, Mediation Works
- May Curtis
- Jessie Feinstein, Development Worker for the Gangs and Territorialism Project, LEAP
- Jack Griffin, Waverley Community Mediation Service
- Paul Holder
- Marian Liebmann
- Ian McDonough, SACRO
- Andrew McLean, Service Development Officer, Mediation UK
- John Marshall, Head of Grants Unit, Home Office Active Community Unit
- Elena Noel, Southwark Mediation Centre
- Helen Prior, Director, Mediation Wales
- Les Platt, Sunderland Mediation
- Richard Shaw, Face to Face Mediation (Herefordshire)
- Anne-Marie Smout, Mediation Sheffield
- Jan Stokes Carter, Mediation in Action

INTRODUCTION AND SCOPE OF THIS REVIEW

This review is designed to give a straightforward introduction to the field of neighbourhood mediation in England, Wales and Scotland: how mediation is provided and funded, who makes use of it, and how standards are set and maintained. Although this is a review of current practice, we have identified in the final chapter the trends, opportunities and tensions that are likely to face this sector over the coming few years.

In referring to community mediation, the Joseph Rowntree Foundation was primarily interested in mediation within local communities and outside legal and justice systems. The Foundation excluded victim–offender and family mediation from the review because of its existing work and knowledge of these areas. Peer mediation was also excluded because of Framework's recent research in this field (Gray, 2001), and mediation in Northern Ireland was excluded because of the conflict resolution work in this region by the Joseph Rowntree Charitable Trust.

In writing this review, we have assumed a basic knowledge of the mediation process. So, we have not provided detailed analysis of the application of mediation to neighbour disputes, except where this helps in identifying differences in current service provision. Similarly, we have not set out a history of the development of mediation in this country, again except when this helps illuminate current practice.

At times, it has been difficult within the review to deal separately with key issues facing local mediation services. For example, issues of quality, success criteria, funding and sources of referrals are all intimately linked. We have therefore sometimes had to make decisions as to where issues such as these are substantively dealt with in the review; we hope, nevertheless, that we have produced an informative and readable study.

The review was carried out by three members of Framework. Set up in 1985, Framework was one of the earliest consultancy networks to operate solely within the not-for-profit sector. The consultancy skills required by this sector are specific to its underpinning values. Our aim is to meet the needs of organisations that serve the community, often with a brief to redress inequality, disadvantage or discrimination. The accumulated knowledge of 17 years' practice means that we are familiar with many of the dilemmas and difficulties faced by those in the voluntary and statutory sectors. The three Framework consultants – John Gray, Moira Halliday and Andrew Woodgate – all brought their specific experience from extensive work within the field of community mediation. Framework can be contacted at www.framework.org.uk

Many individuals and mediation services have assisted our preparation of this review by generously giving their time, knowledge and experience. They are identified in the Acknowledgements and we here record our thanks to them.

Executive summary

The overall picture emerging from this review is of a diverse sector responding with skills, imagination and sensitivity to local community conflict. Mediation services are funded and supported by broad coalitions of agency, community and charitable sources, and by and large have good reputations both with their agency partners and local people. Growing statutory opportunities (via legislation and funding) are leading to a greater mainstreaming of mediation and mediation-like activities. A few services have significant levels of income whereas rather more are much smaller; many services face difficulties of securing medium-term and longer-term sustainability.

Chapter 1 Definitions of community mediation

Community mediation is defined by the sector either in inclusive terms (by reference to the services provided to the community) or in exclusive terms (mediation that is not commercial or family mediation). In either case, it refers to neighbour, victim–offender and peer mediation, and conflict resolution in schools. Sometimes, 'community mediation' is used when referring to 'neighbour mediation', which has led to confusion within the sector. 'Neighbour mediation' is used in this review to distinguish mediation between local residents from victim–offender and peer mediation, which are the other strands of mediation included within community mediation.

Neighbour mediation is developing from a traditional intervention between two households into a dynamic engagement with a broad range of neighbour conflicts loosely characterised by the fact that the parties (local groups or communities of residents) live in reasonably close proximity and are facing conflicts that arise by virtue of living within that residential area.

There is increasing confusion over the use of mediation and conciliation, and services have a responsibility to government and funders to be explicit in their understanding of what mediation entails, and how it differs from other forms of alternative dispute resolution.

Mediation is being used to resolve many other disputes beyond neighbourhood conflict, and community mediation services are involved in mediating some of these disputes. As well as victim–offender and peer mediation, areas of particular growth for services include special educational needs mediation, health service conciliation and workplace mediation. Mediation UK has recently become the national provider of disability conciliation, in partnership with the Disability Rights Commission.

Chapter 2 Service providers

Constitutionally, neighbour mediation services are either managed 'in-house' within another agency (usually a local authority) or are independent charities. Approximately 90 per cent of Mediation UK's service members are charities, with local authority mediation services making up the majority of the in-house services – although other agency in-house services do exist.

Local authorities may prefer to set up their own in-house mediation service rather than having less control over an independent charity. However, the decline in the levels of local authority housing stock (through Right to Buy and stock transfers) may in future limit the numbers of local authority in-house services. This decline in stock is significant for both in-house and independent services, because the less stock a housing authority holds, the less impetus there is for the housing department within that authority to continue to fund a local neighbour mediation service.

The voluntary basis of mediation has meant that most services use volunteer mediators to provide the mediation. There is an increasing trend, however, for services to make use of paid mediators in order to meet caseload demands and service level agreement targets.

Chapter 3 Service provision

Mediation UK has 174 service members, 140 of which deliver neighbour mediation. Approximately 50 per cent of the population has access to a local mediation service; 16,000 disputes a year are estimated to be referred to services, of which 12,000 are accepted as suitable for mediation. A total of 3,500 mediators nationwide are involved in neighbour dispute mediation.

Housing officers (51 per cent) and police (9 per cent) are the main agency referrers of neighbour disputes; overall, a further 30 per cent of cases are self-referrals where one party initiates contact with the mediation service.

Although services differ in their definitions of individual disputes, noise (45 per cent) and violence (37 per cent) dominate the range of issues dealt with by mediation services. Only 2 per cent of cases are reported to involve racial harassment, but many services screen out such cases as not being suitable for mediation. However, a few services have found ways of engaging with serious violent conflict.

Despite the universal image of mediation, nationally only 12 per cent of cases end up in a joint meeting of neighbours. Some cases are resolved without the need for a joint meeting and, in other cases, an agreement is brokered by mediators moving back and forth between the parties. There is confusion within the sector about the use of the phrase 'shuttle mediation'. Most services would like to encourage greater numbers of people to meet with their neighbour in mediation, but find difficulties in achieving this. Where parties do meet together, national success in producing a full agreement rises from 19 per cent to 90 per cent.

Assessment services have developed as a way of encouraging better referrals and higher numbers of joint meetings.

Nationwide, services are responding to a vast range of community conflicts. Imaginative ideas are being tested, and creative agency and community partnerships are being formed.

Chapter 4 Service users

As a general rule, services tend to be more representative of their local communities in terms of service users than mediators. Some services conduct quite in-depth monitoring of service users – gender, age and employment status, as well as ethnic background.

Although exact figures are not available, mediation is more likely to be accessed by neighbours from lower socio-economic groups; and women are more likely than men to be parties to a mediated dispute.

Services have several interesting examples of working with children within the mediation process. Most services encourage the participation of children in mediation, including at joint meetings.

Executive summary

Chapter 5 Service funders

Local authorities and other agencies, charitable grants and a growing reliance on self-generated income provide the main income streams for neighbour mediation services. There is a vast diversity of service income levels across the country – services ranged in their income from £3,623 to over £233,000 per year. Self-generated income is a growing income stream, with one service raising over £41,000 in this way.

The community mediation sector has a strong commitment to providing mediation free at the point of use. This is based on a variety of reasons: a moral commitment within the sector that mediation should be freely and widely available within local communities; not everyone is personally responsible for being in dispute with their neighbour, because usually people cannot choose who their neighbours are; and, more pragmatically, because it would be difficult for mediation services to raise sufficient income by charging the parties themselves.

Many services find difficulty in ensuring their medium- and longer-term financial sustainability. There are opportunities for local capacity-building that can also be used to promote service sustainability.

Local authority funding, whether restricted (Housing Revenue Account) or unrestricted (General Fund), brings dilemmas for services about encouraging open access to mediation. Housing Revenue Account and housing association grants are limited to tenants of that particular landlord, but additional General Fund monies leave the service open to the charge that local tenants are then paying for the service twice. Best Value is likely to have a significant impact both on the level of funding available from local authorities and on the lengths that local services will have to go to in order to demonstrate their cost-effectiveness.

Research into the cost-effectiveness of mediation is still incomplete, and services lack information that conclusively proves the value of mediation in neighbour disputes. Some 30 per cent of mediated disputes reach a full or partial solution; this percentage reflects the difficulty of trying to resolve what can be very entrenched or complex conflicts.

There is central government funding of Mediation UK, but this seems to be in spite of rather than because of greater government enthusiasm for promoting alternative forms of dispute resolution. Services and service networks within Wales and Scotland are developing constructive relationships with their respective devolved governmental structures.

Chapter 6 Quality standards

The introduction of the Community Legal Service's Quality Mark has dramatically altered Mediation UK's work on quality standards within the last two years. Services have been reluctant to take up Mediation UK sponsored quality systems, and it is unclear how far that reluctance will extend to the Quality Mark. While a number of services are preparing to apply for the Quality Mark, there is also substantial objection to this new quality initiative. These objections are based either on practical concerns about the time and effort that is generally believed to be involved in making an application, or on more ethical concerns that the Quality Mark will not result in improved service quality and, rather, has the effect of restricting service creativity and innovation.

At least one service has developed its own quality system, geared to the needs of the service and its funders and volunteers.

Chapter 7 Future trends and tensions

The following trends can be identified as facing the community mediation sector over the coming years:

- service sustainability and capacity-building
- engagement in violent conflict
- the future of Mediation UK's role in representing victim–offender mediation
- the impact of the Quality Mark
- the growing use of paid mediators to deliver neighbour mediation
- responding to academic criticisms of mediation.

1 Definitions of community mediation

Definitions of community mediation

We found that services and Mediation UK defined community mediation either by inclusion or exclusion – namely, by what community mediation includes or what it excludes. In practice, both definitions come to the same result: community mediation is generally held to include three basic areas of provision: victim–offender mediation; peer mediation/conflict resolution work in schools; and neighbour mediation between households and residents of a particular locality.

Definition by inclusion

Taken inclusively, community mediation is defined by reference to its values and practice. The need for mediation is taken to spring from the local community, and the mediation is traditionally provided by members of that community (typically by volunteer mediators). This definition clearly fits the traditional model of neighbour mediation: a dispute between two households about a conflict or disagreement specific to those households.

As this review shows, community mediation services are interpreting neighbour mediation to be capable of addressing a much broader range of community conflicts. Disagreements are being addressed that involve different communities, or multi-party disputes made up of many residents who are in conflict because of the societal, economic or amenity constraints within that locality.

Most mediation services would also assume that community mediation is free at the point of use (in contrast to non-legally aided commercial, civil and family mediation).

Although victim–offender and peer mediation were excluded from the remit of the review, this inclusive definition would for most services include these two forms of mediation as well as neighbour mediation. Victim–offender mediation is understood to take place within a context of relationships involving the victim, offender and the wider local community within which the offence took place. As for peer mediation and other conflict resolution work with schoolchildren, schools are a microcosm of their local community, and working in schools can be a natural extension by neighbour mediation services of their work within their local community.

Only one criticism was made to us of this inclusive definition and it focused on the word, community. Mediation within a community sometimes is not actually provided by that community – for example, city-wide or rural services that do not have volunteers from all parts of the area they serve. Further, it is usually more accurate to describe a large mixed population as a collection of communities rather than as one community; moreover, people frequently define themselves according to which community – or communities – they belong to.

In spite of this criticism, overall the inclusive approach is accurate and has the advantage of building the values of mediation into the intended service provision.

Definition by exclusion

Historically, community mediation has also been defined by the fact that some significant areas of mediation – family and commercial – had evolved separate national representative bodies. In overseeing community mediation, therefore, Mediation UK was effectively responsible for mediation which is 'not family or commercial'. As Mediation UK's service membership consists almost wholly of neighbour, victim–offender and peer mediation services, this exclusive definition thus produces the same result as the inclusive approach.

Confusion arises as to what is meant by community mediation because it is sometimes used to refer just to neighbour mediation – and not victim–offender or peer. Mediation UK has at times been guilty of this double use of the phrase. That community mediation could be seen as synonymous to neighbour mediation is because, historically, neighbour mediation has been the easiest of the three to fund, which is why it has developed much more widely than the other forms of service provision represented by Mediation UK.

Community mediation and neighbour mediation within this review

Although community mediation is generally agreed to include victim–offender and peer mediation, yet these two areas of mediation were not included within the review; we therefore use 'community mediation' in this review to mean services represented by Mediation UK (covering neighbour dispute, peer mediation and victim–offender) and 'neighbour mediation' to mean disputes among local residents. As we have already indicated within the inclusive definition, neighbour mediation is rapidly developing from just mediating between two adjoining households into a dynamic engagement with a wide range of community disputes (see Chapter 3, section on 'Other forms of neighbourhood-based mediation').

Conciliation vs. mediation

One other linguistic confusion needs to be cleared up at this stage.

Mediation is traditionally used in the UK to describe a process of third party assisted negotiation – i.e. inviting an outsider to help the negotiation of a resolution of the conflict. Increasingly, conciliation is being used in a number of statutory or public sector processes to identify a process identical to mediation. Examples include Disability Rights Conciliation, and conciliation in the health service between patients and the NHS.

However, differences exist in the usage of mediation or conciliation, differences that focus mainly on the authority of the mediator to suggest solutions and advise the parties on legal or practical issues. Most neighbour mediation services would understand mediators as having no power to suggest and/or advise, whereas conciliators would have more freedom of movement (especially in a rights-based dispute resolution process, such as that operated by the Disability Conciliation Service). However, there are examples (principally outside the neighbour mediation field), where a process of mediation is understood to describe mediators who can advise and suggest, and conciliation implies a strictly hands-off approach.

Confusingly, the Arbitration, Conciliation and Advisory Service refers to conciliation, dispute mediation and advisory mediation as three different strands of its work within employment dispute resolution. Dispute mediation is described as being more formal than conciliation, as terms of reference need to be agreed in advance and the process results in the mediator making formal recommendations. More details can be found in Liebmann (2000, Chapter 10).

The consequences of this difference in usage mean that, while community mediation services refer to mediation and between them understand what each other means, new statutory processes and some other dispute resolution agencies do not know what services mean by mediation, and instead sometimes use conciliation. The dilemma is that mediation best describes what services do, but they are under pressure to offer conciliation in order to take advantage of government funding opportunities.

A significant step forward would be for national consensus (including government and legislation) on the difference between mediation and conciliation. As this consensus is unlikely to emerge, mediation services have a clear responsibility to promote the correct usage of mediation wherever possible. While differences in mediation do exist between individual services, in reality the similarity of provision would enable a substantially cohesive statement of practice to be drawn up.

Mediation can be more easily contrasted with arbitration, which gives power to a third party to judge the dispute and to recommend or impose a solution. No examples emerged during this of any community mediation service that offers the combination of mediation and arbitration that has been practised in the USA, where the mediator, should she or he feel that a mediated resolution is unlikely, may decide explicitly to switch roles and arbitrate the dispute.

Mapping of other forms of mediation

The definition of mediation given at the beginning of this chapter (third party assisted negotiation) acknowledges mediation to be a broad conflict intervention mechanism. It has been growing in its use within Britain, particularly over the last 20 years. What follows is an attempt to summarise the many areas in which mediation (including conciliation) occurs, identifying whether community mediation services are involved in service provision.

Family

Provided by a national network of family mediation services, primarily mediating separating couples on children and financial issues. This area of mediation is not included within the scope of this review, although a few community mediation services do provide both neighbour and family mediation.

Family other than mediation for separating couples

An example is Blackpool Mediation Service, which has received funding from the local Primary Care Group to provide a family mediation project – that is, mediating between young people and their parents. Similarly, Bliss Community Mediation Service (Blyth Valley, Northumberland) offers mediation in such family circumstances as a young person running away from home, making a move away from home constructive, and disputes between young people and their parents or grandparents.

Special educational needs (SEN)

The new SEN Code of Practice requires local education authorities (LEAs) to make mediation-like disagreement resolution available within the Statementing process. Significant government funding has been released to regional SEN Partnerships that have been established across England, and many community mediation services are seeking training on SEN mediation in order to bid for mediation either from the Partnerships or directly from LEAs.

Definitions of community mediation

Disability Conciliation Service

Established under the Disability Discrimination Act 1995. Mediation UK has been awarded the tender for providing conciliation between service users and service providers under Part 3 of the Act, in collaboration with the newly established Disability Rights Commission. Conciliation is recommended by the Commission when no test-case principle is involved. Mediation is provided by a national team of conciliators trained and supported by Mediation UK's Disability Conciliation Service.

The multicultural Elder Mediation Project

The multicultural Elder Mediation Project (EMP) works independently and in collaboration with community mediation services to promote mediation as a tool 'to make a valuable contribution to the welfare of those who suffer from social conflicts associated with their ageing, disabilities and mental frailties' (Liebmann, 2000, Chapter 14).

Centre for Effective Dispute Resolution/NCVO mediation service for voluntary organisations

The National Council for Voluntary Organisations (NCVO) was established to champion the cause of the voluntary sector and work to improve its effectiveness. Charities and voluntary organisations encounter the same range of disputes and conflicts as other businesses. Voluntary organisations are also strongly value-based, and may experience intense internal conflicts about directions and policies. Although there may be no immediate financial risk, the drain on support and on people's time may be expensive and the public image of the organisation may be damaged.

The Charities Unit at the Centre for Effective Dispute Resolution (CEDR) is a focus group working with other charities and the NCVO. Mediation had already been used successfully in a number of disputes involving charities and both the NCVO and CEDR saw further scope for development. Mediation helps ensure that the chance of a resolution succeeding in the long term is increased and generally 85 per cent of mediations are settled in one day. Consequently, the Charity Commission is keen that this avenue is explored by the voluntary sector.

CEDR and the NCVO work together to form a joint mediation service. This CEDR/NCVO subsidised service is available to all voluntary organisations and is supported by the Active Community Unit of the Home Office. The scheme offers a five-hour mediation session and is based on a three-tier fee system. An individual organisation pays fees dependent on its size with half of the expense subsidised by the service itself. This means a small organisation can pay as little as £250.

A panel of CEDR mediators was identified for the scheme, drawn from a range of backgrounds including the voluntary sector, law, management consultancy, counselling and training, and the scheme is managed by a CEDR dispute resolution adviser. All the mediators are CEDR accredited, have access to their continued professional development programme and carry professional indemnity insurance.

The Charity Commission is represented on the steering group of the mediation service, as are lawyers, mediators and representatives from NCVO and CEDR.

Stakeholder dialogue/Environment Council

The Environment Council, an independent UK charity, brings together people from all sectors of business, non-governmental organisations, government and the community to develop long-

Definitions of community mediation

term solutions to environmental issues. Paid mediators use a range of techniques based around mediation and dialogue.

One published case study provides an example of stakeholder dialogue in action. This is the 'community brainstorm' which was run over a three-month period in 1997 after concern over an alleged cluster of leukaemia cases developed in south Newbury. Those involved in the process were concerned local people, media and local government representatives from Newbury District Council. A budget of £1,500 for the process was provided by the local authority.

Local people had identified a cluster of cases, which was confirmed by a health authority investigation. The Head of Environmental Health recognised that a facilitated meeting would offer the best way of hearing local concerns regarding the possible causes for the cluster. The local community would have a key role in shaping the way forwards.

The process started with setting up a facilitated public meeting from which flowed an ongoing working group. The aim of the meeting was to involve as many locals as possible in brainstorming the possible causes for the cluster and then to agree a way forward. Allowing the public to raise their concerns in a non-judgemental forum that was not dominated by 'experts' led to the success of the meeting. Realistic paths for the investigations to follow were discussed and a working party was composed from those present to take the work forward. This has continued to meet and is consulted by the District Council and other bodies.

No environmental cause of the leukaemia has yet been identified. However, the work produced within the group is of extreme value and has recently been presented to an intergovernmental conference on health in London.

The facilitated process used for the meetings had a number of advantages:

- It was an effective way of managing a meeting which could potentially have had over 100 people present.
- It provided a safe, non-critical environment, which allowed all participants to have a say and more people to participate than otherwise may have.
- Local people felt the experts were listening to what they had to say, rather than the other way around.
- As a result, they felt engaged in an issue affecting their community.
- The resulting working group is independent from, although supported by, the Council.
- Facilitation of the meeting by an independent third party ensured that no 'side' or group of people was favoured; all were treated equally.

Central London County Court project

Set up as a pilot in 1996, the scheme gives litigants the chance to have the case mediated at an early stage rather than following the lengthy court procedure. Mediators are provided primarily from the commercially/legally based Centre for Dispute Resolution. Mediation is available for cases above the 'small claims' limit, as claims below that limit are already subject to a more informal process of arbitration by District Judges. Strongly supported by Master of the Rolls Lord Woolf, the pilot builds on the determination of the Lord Chancellor's Department to encourage alternative dispute resolution within the civil justice system (*Modernising Justice* White Paper, December 1998). The Central London County Court scheme is to be extended to the Bristol and Leeds County Courts. See Genn (1999) for an evaluation of the Central London County Court scheme.

Other legal disputes

Informal mediation is being provided by some community mediation services for disputes over wills and probate, private landlord and tenant, and deeds of covenant.

Workplace mediation

Particularly within the public sector, there is growing use of mediation to resolve disputes between employers and employees, and between colleagues and within work teams. Workplace mediation traditionally does not extend to large-scale resourcing disputes, nor to disputes about conditions of service and employment covered by national agreements. Further impetus in this field has been provided by the Employment Rights (Dispute Resolution) Act 1999, which introduces a voluntary binding arbitration procedure into Employment Tribunals procedures, as well as giving new powers to tribunal chairs to refer cases back to the employer. Further information is provided in Liebmann (2000, Chapter 11).

NHS conciliation

Fitting into NHS and Trust complaints procedures, some community mediation services are negotiating contracts to mediate disputes between patients and health providers.

Other complaints processes

Similarly, statutory complaints processes, such as those within social services and children's services, are looking to mediation to provide alternative methods of investigation and dispute resolution, and some community mediation services have benefited from negotiating contracts to provide the mediation required.

Arbitration, Advisory and Conciliation Service

Established in 1974, the Arbitration, Advisory and Conciliation Service (ACAS) exists to improve the performance and effectiveness of organisations by providing an independent and impartial service to prevent and resolve disputes, and to build harmonious relationships at work. As well as conciliation and arbitration of disputes, ACAS also provides both advisory and dispute mediation for organisation-wide disputes and individual employment rights cases. Further information is provided in Liebmann (2000, Chapter 10).

Peer mediation and work in schools

This is not included within the scope of this review. In summary, work by community mediation services focuses either on training children to mediate disputes among other children (their peers), and/or on communication skills, exploring feelings and self-expression, conflict awareness and conflict resolution skills, and helping the school develop an effective culture of conflict management. For neighbour mediation services, peer mediation is a natural area of development: schools are a microcosm of the wider neighbourhood and, in working with children, a service can hope to encourage effective conflict resolution in the neighbours and householders of tomorrow.

Victim–offender mediation

This is also not included in the scope of this review. Pioneered by West Yorkshire Probation Service, mediation and reparation between victim and offender has led to reduced offending rates and to enabling the victim to put the offence behind them. This field has been revolutionised by the 1998 Crime and Disorder Act's introduction of Youth Offending Teams and Reparation

Orders for young offenders, with victim–offender mediation being provided either by community mediation services or from staff located within the Youth Offending Team. Referral Orders will provide a further opportunity for the community at large, as well as the offender's family to be involved in developing a contract that may include both reparation to the victim and conditions to prevent reoffending.

Bridge Builders

Part of the London Mennonite Centre, Bridge Builders provides mediation of congregational conflict and interpersonal mediation between church members. A structured but adaptable process mixes mediation, recommendation-making and consultancy to provide a range of tools for congregational intervention. Representative working groups are established to help streamline work with the whole congregation. The process typically takes between six and nine months. There is a basic charge of around £4,000, although Bridge Builders charged £7,000 for mediating a congregational conflict in 2000, which required 300 mediator-hours.

2 SERVICE PROVIDERS

This chapter looks at mediation services' legal frameworks. It also identifies opposing trends that may influence the future of local authority involvement in managing mediation services.

Models of provision

There are two models, which together make up the vast majority of neighbour mediation provision in England, Wales and Scotland.

Model 1

An independent charity registered with the Charity Commissioners and managed by a management board of trustees, usually made up of representatives from local funding agencies, referrers, other significant community agencies relevant to the service and (to a greater or lesser extent) representation from the team of mediators. Although exact figures are not available from Mediation UK, this model of service provision makes up at least 85 per cent of Mediation UK's neighbour mediation member services.

Model 2

An agency-managed service, usually referred to as 'in-house'. The managing agency is typically a local authority, but it is important to stress that the term in-house does not imply that the service is necessarily limited to tenants of the managing agency, nor that the independence of its mediation is compromised by being within the agency.

Mediation UK estimates that 10 per cent of its member services are in-house. Even though the service may still use volunteers, staff are agency employees and line management is provided from within the Council.

Invariably, Housing Services are the managing department; typical examples include Bradford Mediation, Bolton Mediation and South Lanarkshire. City of York Council's service Face to Face is located in a combined Housing and Social Care department, but line management is provided through Strategic Services rather than through Housing Services to promote the service's independence from its Housing Revenue Account funding.

The other main examples of agency-managed services are those managed by SACRO (Safeguarding Communities – Reducing Offending) in Scotland. SACRO aims to promote safer communities by 'providing a range of effective services across Scotland to reduce conflict and offending and by influencing criminal justice and social policy' (McDonough, 2001a, 2001b). Within this brief, SACRO manages both victim–offender and neighbour mediation services across Scotland. Individual services are responsible for their day-to-day running; SACRO provides human resources and personnel functions, sets policy across the range of its services, and oversees financial accounting of its member services.

There are other examples of charitable organisations that include in-house neighbour mediation within their other activities: for example, Hastings and Rother Mediation Service (part of Hastings and Rother Citizens Advice Bureau); and a mediation service provided by a legal advice charity (Norwich and District Legal Services).

The future of local authority managed services

Should a local authority want to support the creation of a new mediation service in its area, some authorities will choose to retain a measure of control by setting up their own in-house service, rather than helping to create an independent service in the voluntary sector (Face to Face, City of York Council's service, is the product of a deliberate decision to set up an in-house rather than an independent service, and was explicitly modelled on Bolton Metropolitan District Council Neighbour Dispute Service). Such a decision retains within the local authority the management and development of the service, as well as tying the service more closely in with the authority's landlord functions.

However, there are two trends that now mitigate against local authorities choosing to establish in-house services. Because they both reduce the level of local authority housing stock, both trends are likely to limit local authority involvement in funding neighbour mediation generally.

First, the Right to Buy policy operates a slow but steady drain on the number of council tenant properties.

Second, and on a larger scale, the growth in the last two years of local authority housing stock transfers could prove to have a significant impact on in-house services. Sunderland Mediation, an in-house service, stayed within the City Health and Housing department following a transfer in April 2001 of the authority's housing stock to the independent Sunderland Housing Group. Future service funding (in part guaranteed for 2002–03 from the General Fund) therefore depends on the willingness of the new Housing Group, along with other social landlords, to fund mediation in the city.

Sunderland is the only in-house service that we are aware of to have faced the consequences of stock transfer, although

Birmingham City Council's mediation service may be affected if the Council's application to transfer stock is approved. However, should stock transfer become significant nationwide, then independent services will also definitely be affected as housing stock moves from the authority to independent housing associations. We became aware of stock transfers being considered in two areas covered by independent community mediation services, Kirklees and Peterborough, but the real number is likely to be far higher.

Paid and volunteer mediators

A significant number of services that we contacted have begun paying mediators to deliver neighbour mediation or were considering doing so.

Southwark Mediation Centre is an example of a service that employs full-time mediators (it has six full-time mediators, together with two part-time mediators and a team of eight volunteer mediators). In 1997–98, Southwark's average gross full-time salary for mediators was £23,783 (Mulcahy with Summerfield, 2001).

For other services, payment is usually on a sessional or hourly basis. The one rate of pay that we were quoted was £10.50 per hour for mediating (likely to be increased to £12.50), with a lower hourly rate for administration and case management time.

Of the services we spoke to, the rationale for paying mediators was usually to ensure that the service would meet service delivery targets. Identified difficulties included a shortage of volunteers, or excessive workload, or to ensure daytime mediator availability. In Cardiff, paid mediators carry out initial visits to both sides, so that cases are then handed over to volunteers only when all parties are willing to proceed to mediation.

It is common for mediation services to have a background of volunteering. Services also frequently discover that neighbours are more impressed by the fact that the mediators are volunteers, and so are contributing their time and skills through personal commitment and experience of the benefits of mediation rather than because they are paid to do so. This 'moral high ground' can help to build the neighbours' commitment to the mediation process.

Southwark Mediation Centre, however, identified five reasons (Mulcahy with Summerfield, 2001, pp. 31–2) why extensive use of volunteers can be disadvantageous:

1 Volunteers take longer to acquire skills because they often cannot mediate on a regular basis.

2 Council funding provided incentives to increase the use of paid mediators, as the service was reluctant for volunteers to manage cases where the paid staff remained responsible for the progress of their caseload.

3 More work is involved in coordinating volunteers and they do not always commit to being involved in a case from start to finish.

4 Referrers tend to build up a personal relationship with full-time mediators because they can be contacted during the day and cases can be referred more easily to specific mediators.

5 Southwark's increased use of shuttle mediation places demands on mediators which volunteers may not be able to meet.

Service providers

Whether the mediators are paid or voluntary, mediation services are keen to stress that the mediation they provide is still professional. However, there is a debate among services as to whether paid mediation is a compromise of 'traditional' community mediation values – or whether payment is a step towards sector credibility and is thus appropriate recognition of mediators' skills. Regardless of how far 'traditional' values are compromised by payment, according to the services we interviewed, it is clear that the need to meet service level agreement targets is proving to be a driving force.

3 SERVICE PROVISION

This wide-ranging chapter provides a summary of Mediation UK's service membership statistics, and gives an analysis of traditional neighbour mediation cases and the issues of conflict that they involve. This is followed by an examination of the type of mediation used, sector confusion over the phrase 'shuttle mediation' and the development of assessment services. The final section is an introduction to the broad range of other types of neighbourhood-based conflict that neighbour mediation services are engaging with.

An exploration of the outcomes and effectiveness of mediation is located in Chapter 5, funding issues.

Mediation UK's service membership

Mediation UK holds two principal sources of information considered during this review:

1   A collection of neighbour mediation service profile questionnaires, covering the period April 1999 to March 2000. Sixty questionnaires were returned, or 43 per cent of the membership. Mediation UK is now developing a programme of updating these service profiles on a rolling basis when annual subscriptions are renewed.

Service provision

2   The 2001 Community Mediation Dispute Survey, covering 1 April 2000 to 31 March 2001. This is an annual survey of neighbour mediation services and 56 services (40 per cent) responded. (Note the confusing use of 'community mediation' in the title of a survey of services about their involvement in *neighbour* mediation.)

These two sources have been supplemented by individual service Annual Reports (sent to us as part of this review) and telephone interviews with specific services.

From the service profiles held by Mediation UK, it is possible to build up a picture of the range of neighbour mediation activities provided by community mediation services. Of the 174 service members of Mediation UK, 140 deliver neighbour mediation (whether as a sole activity or in conjunction with other activities such as victim–offender or work in schools). The other 34 member services provide peer mediation and/or victim–offender mediation but not neighbour mediation. The number of services is estimated by Mediation UK to provide 50 per cent of the UK population with access to a local mediation service.

Extrapolating from the Community Mediation Dispute Survey results (which may or may not produce an accurate figure), Mediation UK estimates that, for 2000 to 2001, 16,000 requests for mediation were made to local services, of which 12,000 were accepted as being appropriate for mediation.

Some 3,500 people are believed by Mediation UK currently to be involved in mediating disputes in their local community; and, over the years, some 40,000 people have been trained as mediators by their local community mediation service.

An analysis of traditional neighbour mediation cases

How do neighbour disputes reach their local mediation service? The 2001 Community Mediation Dispute Survey identifies the four main referral sources as: housing departments 39 per cent; self-referrals 30 per cent; housing associations 12 per cent; police 9 per cent; followed in decreasing percentages by environmental health departments, advice centres, local councillors, other council departments and legal centres (presumably including solicitors).

Self-referrals are usually at the encouragement of one of the agencies listed above. Because of the voluntary nature of mediation, some services (such as Mediation Sheffield) have a general principle of accepting only self-referrals, not agency referrals, as a way of trying to encourage active neighbour

Table 1 Issues that are the subject of neighbour mediation

Per cent of cases	Issues
45	Noise
20	Abusive behaviour and threats
17	Children's behaviour
17	Boundary or property disputes
15	Anti-social behaviour
6	Cars, parking, vehicle repairs
5	Untidiness, gardens, rubbish, smells
5	Animals (including pets)
2	Racial harassment
2	DIY, building work
2	Family or relationship disputes
<1	Mental health/care in the community
7	Other issues

Note: the percentage total comes to well over 100 per cent, as many disputes involve more than one issue and neighbours often have very different views as to what the dispute is about.

Source: Mediation UK's Annual Community Mediation Dispute Survey 2001.

Service provision

participation right from the start of the mediation process.

The issues that are the subject of neighbour mediation are identified in Table 1.

Interpretation of Table 1 requires some care.

1. These statistics depend on how each service defines the issues involved – for example, abusive threats and behaviour might easily be defined by a different service as children's behaviour, anti-social behaviour and/or racial harassment.

2. The phrase, 'anti-social behaviour', does not in any sense refer to a legal definition of what behaviour counts as anti-social (as used for the making of an Anti-social Behaviour Order or by a social landlord deciding to apply for an eviction order or serving Notice to Seek Possession).

3. Racial harassment featuring as 2 per cent of cases should not be taken to imply that racial harassment features in only 2 per cent of *all* neighbour disputes. The reason for this is that many services screen out cases of serious illegality. Typically, this relates to cases where one party is alleged to be drug-dealing, but cases of serious violence – including racial harassment – may also be deemed by the service to be inappropriate (or unsafe) for mediators to be involved, and instead to be more appropriate for police action. If these cases are screened out, they will not feature in the list of issues mediated by the service.

Nevertheless, in terms of issues, it is clear that nearly half (45 per cent) of cases mediated by neighbour mediation services involve noise; and, taken together, the 'violence' categories of abusive threats and behaviour, anti-social behaviour and racial

Responding to community conflict

harassment feature in 37 per cent of cases. That mediation has proved to be effective in these conflicts accounts for the widespread support by local authorities and police for their local neighbour mediation service.

In many situations of violence, a service may rightly decide not to take on a case, thus not risking the safety of their mediators and/or judging that the situation has advanced too far for mediation to be effective. But some services are looking at using mediation for 'hate crimes', and there are other models for engaging with the causes of violent community conflict.

Hate crimes

Southwark Mediation Centre's Hate Crimes Project, launched in December 2000, is an element within a local partnership that aims to reduce hate crimes incidents, develop confidence in the Metropolitan Police's commitment to deal convincingly with hate crime and create sustainable structures to tackle intolerance within the community. Hate crimes refers to a dispute or committed offence motivated by the race or sexual identify of those involved.

Southwark Mediation Centre's project uses both direct and indirect mediation, with a particular aim of the mediator to enlighten the parties about diversity, exploring their attitudes to differences in race, culture, ethnicity and sexuality. Disputes have involved both just two households and also larger multi-party disputes, and there is an increase in cases involving children, referred by beat police officers linked to local schools. The dispute may involve anti-social behaviour, damage to property, arson or assault – exactly the kinds of case histories that most neighbour mediation services would turn away or refer on. The project has received positive agency feedback both on the rates of resolution and a reduction in reoffending.

Service provision

The two-year project is funded as part of a £668,000 grant from the Home Office's Crime Reduction Programme to the 'Police, Partners and Community Together in Southwark' partnership, a Targeted Police Initiative developed by the Southwark Police Partnership Scheme. There is close liaison between the project and the Police Community Unit, a specialist team tackling race and homophobic crime, domestic violence and crimes against vulnerable people in Southwark.

Gangs and territorialism

LEAP Confronting Conflict has a three-year project looking at the social implications of the growth of youth gangs and territorialism in the UK. The first year has been mainly involved in contacting agencies and young people, and the project is now taking decisions on how to meet the aims of the project, which are: to map approaches to street crimes and intergroup conflicts among severely marginalised young people; to develop and test innovative ways of reintegrating young people involved in street gangs (including large group or whole community mediation); and to disseminate findings and publication of a training manual.

Already the research has challenged assumptions that gangs are established groups into which young people are 'initiated' in order to commit criminal acts or defend a 'territory'. Rather, gangs tend to be loose associations of young people, bored and with very little to do, and who are characterised by having very little access to ways of achieving a high social status (such as a job, or good education). The gang, and the validation by one's peers that it offers, is an alternative way of creating individual status. Gang members are not necessarily committing crimes, although fights may be common, but by being in groups (frequently after dark) they tap into community

continued overleaf

and media perceptions of young people out of society's control. They are often stopped by the police, although not necessarily arrested. Racial tensions and minority intercommunal conflicts are often reflected within the gang and between the gang and the local community.

Three key themes have emerged from the project's first year:

- The role of the 'anti-hero' is deemed by gang members to be worthy and literally worth fighting for. The project is looking at ways in which this desired status can be explored and challenged.
- There are key issues around space and territorialism which link to perceptions of ownership that the project is keen to explore.
- The transitions young people face offer opportunities – rarely provided – for them to include leadership qualities within their personal development.

The development worker within the project who we spoke to was clear that many community mediation services would have the skills – if not necessarily the commitment – to engage in similar work within their local community.

The project is funded by a grant of £47,670 for three years from the Diana, Princess of Wales Memorial Fund.

Community and inter-agency facilitation

In demonstrating a level of engagement between mediating violent conflicts and ignoring them altogether, Mediation Oxfordshire was invited to facilitate a meeting prompted by the 11 September attacks. Local minority community representatives and members shared information, areas of tension and joint working opportunities with staff from local statutory agencies.

Aik Saath: togetherness

Interethnic tensions within Slough's Asian populations brought unwelcome media attention and growing negative perceptions of Asian young people. Work with the young people produced the idea for a conflict resolution programme, which was funded by Channel 4 television and supported by the local Council. An international facilitator was involved to support young people in meeting with the Council; training in conflict resolution and presentation skills followed, after which young people took their skills to community groups, youth clubs and schools.

The community sees the young people as a valuable resource and there has been a noticeable increase in Asian young people accessing services and information. The project has led to a much better understanding of issues within the community and tension has dramatically reduced. (Gowan, 2000, p. 29)

Comment: although Aik Saath is not part of a community mediation service, the activities described could well fit into a service's engagement with its local communities.

What type of mediation is used?

Table 2 indicates the types of mediation used by services.

Again, care is needed to understand the figures shown in Table 2, as services were asked to tick any box that applied to each case, so a case which went to a face-to-face meeting (or joint meeting) would almost certainly also include visits to both sides. The universal image of mediation is of a joint meeting: the parties sitting down in the same room together with mediators. And, while some services report joint meeting percentages of over 20 per cent, the national picture reveals joint meetings in fact take place in a comparatively low number of cases.

Table 2 Types of mediation used

Type	Per cent
Face-to-face	12
Shuttle*	16
Visit to first party	31
Visit to second party	19
Telephone contact first party	17
Telephone contact second party	9
Other	11

*See the next section of this chapter for an analysis of this term.
Source: Mediation UK's Annual Community Mediation Dispute Survey 2001.

The reasons for this low percentage are easier to identify than to remedy. Indeed, sometimes no remedy is needed, as some cases do not need a joint meeting: mediator intervention, sometimes only with one party, is enough either for the party to re-evaluate the seriousness of the dispute or for one party to approach the other directly to resolve things there and then.

Frequently, however, the refusal to go to a joint meeting is for more negative reasons. People may have a legitimate fear of meeting their neighbour given the history of the dispute, although most services would formally or informally carry out some kind of risk assessment before arranging a joint meeting. Neighbours may be reluctant to take what is usually seen as the most challenging step within the mediation process, implying therefore either an imperfect commitment to the process or a lack of trust in the mediators to manage it to a successful conclusion.

Mediators' experience shows that the most resistance initially to the idea of mediation arises because of the parties' expectation that they will have to meet their neighbour. However, most services want to increase the number of face-to-face mediations because they know it significantly boosts the chance of a lasting full agreement. From services' Annual Reports, we have learnt that the Mediation UK figure for full agreement rises from 19 per cent nationally across *all* cases to over 90 per cent in those cases that go to a joint meeting. Further information on success outcomes of mediation is provided in Chapter 5.

Shuttle mediation – a contradiction of usage

At least three distinct definitions of shuttle are widely prevalent among mediation services. In all three situations, the shuttle technique means separate contact between the mediators and the parties.

Definition 1

Shuttle mediation is used to refer to a process that arises either because the parties have declined to meet or because the service does not want to arrange a joint meeting because of safety or other concerns. Shuttle mediation is therefore chosen as the next best prospective way of getting to a satisfactory resolution. In attempting to broker an agreement over the course of a pre-arranged few hours, the mediators shuttle frequently between the parties who are either in their own homes or (as in Northern Ireland type proximity talks) in adjoining rooms at a neutral venue. Whatever the format, the mediators use the shuttling to clarify issues and seek specific wording of an agreement (either written or verbal). Services that use this definition of shuttle mediation usually make a conscious decision during the case not to try further to encourage a joint meeting and instead agree with or declare openly to the parties that they are now mediating on the basis of shuttle mediation.

Definition 2

Shuttle mediation can also be used to refer to a process of reaching a specifically worded agreement, but one that is arrived at during a series of visits over a period of weeks rather than going backwards and forwards within a limited time during one day. In this situation, the parties have usually not yet declined to meet, but reluctance to make a firm decision leads the service to seek agreement in another way. Again, the outcome is a specifically worded agreement, but is more likely to be verbal than written.

Definition 3

Lastly, shuttle mediation is also used to refer to *any* contact between the mediators and parties, whether prior to a joint meeting or where no joint meeting takes place. Rather than looking to reach an agreement of the whole dispute, the mediators include within the shuttle process the standard tasks of explaining what mediation is, hearing about the issues in dispute, relaying information between the parties and encouraging both to agree to come to a joint meeting.

The range of usage is bewildering and at times leads to confusion in discussions between services. Some of them avoid the word shuttle altogether and instead use the terms direct and indirect mediation to refer respectively to joint meetings and shuttle/non-face-to-face contact. Direct and indirect are at least consistent terms and avoid the jargon and confusion arising from shuttle. Clarity on the meaning of shuttle is important, because the term conceals fundamental differences about the role of the mediators within the process.

What services also need to be wary of is the occasional tendency to use the single word mediation to refer to a joint meeting. A typical context would be: 'we met both sides separately and they decided to go to mediation'. Most mediation services claim that the mediation process is effectively under way when mediators have contact with the separate sides in the dispute, because the mediators can then justifiably claim to be positioned between the parties. To use the word mediation just for a joint meeting risks missing out on the valuable communication and clarifying between the parties that mediators facilitate through separate contact.

Pre-mediation activities – the development of assessment services

All services need to spend time with clients to ensure that they understand mediation properly and are committed to using the service. Many services have found that volunteer mediators can become demotivated if they are too frequently asked to spend their time meeting with neighbours who do not in fact want mediation.

Some services have responded to this by involving staff in initial visits to clients, so that mediators only visit neighbours who are wanting to use the service. However, a pioneering development by Leicestershire Mediation Service (LMS) took this initial assessment work a significant stage further.

Spurred on by the low quality of many of its referrals and a corresponding drop in volunteer mediator morale, LMS developed a pilot partnership with one of the city's area housing offices. Funded by the Council's housing department, *all* cases of neighbour nuisance that were reported to the housing office, except the most serious violent or breach of tenancy cases, would be automatically referred to the mediation service. The service, using a team of trained staff and volunteer assessors, would then visit both sides (including initiating contact with the party complained about) to assess the case and, where appropriate, to advise the parties on action they could take. The assessment resulted in one of four outcomes, depending on the nature of the dispute and the attitudes of the parties: refer back to Housing Services; refer on to another department or agency; no further action; or referral to mediation.

This fourth outcome produced the apparently paradoxical situation of the mediation service referring cases to itself. But these referrals were the result of a visit by staff or volunteers who were familiar with mediation, able to judge mediation's suitability and to explain and actively encourage neighbours to follow it through. Both sides would have been visited and would have agreed to mediation, so volunteer mediators could take the case already knowing that both sides were expecting and wanting to hear from them.

LMS noted an improvement in the quality of referrals and the number of joint meetings rose; thus the quality of outcomes to mediation increased along with mediator satisfaction. The pilot proved to be so successful that the scheme was expanded to cover all the Council's area housing offices. The workload of assessment visits was extremely high, with upwards of 20 faxed referrals coming in daily at one stage. At least three other neighbour services – New Forest Mediation, Mediation in Action and Bristol Mediation – have put similar assessment services into operation in partnership with their local authority; a similar pilot relationship is running between Charter Housing Association, Mediation Works (Monmouthshire) and Newport Mediation (funded jointly by the housing association and the Welsh Assembly).

Other forms of neighbourhood-based mediation

Neighbour mediation has traditionally meant mediating a dispute primarily involving two adjoining households. However, it is clear that neighbour mediation within the broader community mediation definition is being expanded by services to include other situations of community conflict. Examples of these services that we came across during this review are as follows.

Blackpool Mediation Service

Blackpool Mediation Service has a project in its infancy that will be working with housing associations, landlords with homes in multiple occupation and environmental services to provide not just mediation between neighbours but also between tenants and their landlords.

Edinburgh Community Mediation Service

Edinburgh Community Mediation Service, as well as providing household-to-household mediation, mediates multi-party conflicts involving whole streets or 'stair mediations' (six to eight tenants sharing a common staircase). The service has mediated between two church congregations coming together but each wanting to keep their premises; and has also mediated a conflict involving the prostitute union. The service is teaming up with a community safety group to go into intergenerational mediation focusing on perceived problems of young people hanging around street corners. The intention is to target troublesome areas, and encourage people to take the trouble to learn about different cultures through use of drama and art.

As an alternative to shuttling a written agreement, Edinburgh chooses to provide 'kitchen table mediation': if the mediators get the impression that the parties are ready to meet then the mediators arrange it there and then by bringing next door in. The aim is not to let the structure of the mediation process get in the way of mediating a successful agreement.

Mediation Oxfordshire

Mediation Oxfordshire has facilitated broader community conflicts such as groups of neighbours and a voluntary sector organisation operating in the neighbourhood; between groups of people and a local business; and between different groups in the community (such as children and their parents and other people living near a recreational ground). The service is interested in helping communities (neighbourhoods or others) to manage and find a way through conflict generally as well as specific disputes. The service also gets involved with other community development projects (e.g. the East Oxford Single Regeneration Budget [SRB] and a multi-agency response to racial harassment). Staff were very involved in a recent meeting called in East Oxford to tackle racial taunts against the Muslim community following the 11 September attacks.

Proactive work by Mediation Oxfordshire has been made possible through an outreach worker for the past three years (three days per week, funded by the Lottery). He has worked proactively throughout the area but particularly in three city estates (identified by local authority, police, etc. as most needy). The post has combined information and awareness-raising about mediation with providing basic training to community groups in mediation skills.

Mediation in Kirklees

Mediation in Kirklees has worked in partnership with Inroads, an arm of Catholic Housing Aid Society (CHAS). The project aims to work with young people outside schools to boost their life skills by offering a package of advice, training and financial management skills. Mediation skills are seen as relevant to help young people understand their own behaviour and the consequences it might have on others. Mediation in Kirklees has run two conflict management courses, with future courses dependent on funding.

Fife Community Mediation

Fife Community Mediation has researched the impact of neighbour disputes on health and how resolution of the conflict leads to a corresponding improvement in over half of the disputants.

Newham Conflict and Change Project

Newham Conflict and Change Project's Community Development Team has mapped out how various groups within the Borough (such as faith communities, ethnic minorities and refugees) experience and resolve conflict. As a result of initial research, the team is supporting women's groups and making connections with young people. In collaboration with participating groups, the service aims to produce a manual of culturally appropriate methods of conflict prevention and resolution.

Cardiff Mediation

Cardiff Mediation is considering becoming a 'community conflict sponsor' – that is, an organisation that would identify and name problems as 'conflict'. An example of this at the moment is that some bus services in the city are being cut back because youths stone buses in certain areas. Traditional agencies are failing to get to grips with this problem; the services could well use mediation techniques to bring the various parties together. The new agenda around tenant participation could also prove a fertile ground for mediation approaches.

Bristol Mediation

Bristol Mediation is beginning to offer new community facilitation approaches to resolving conflict as part of the Healthy Living Centre in Knowle West.

Mesh (Mediation Sheffield)

In a move to take mediation further into the heart of local communities within the city it serves, Mesh (Mediation Sheffield) has established four satellite projects across the city. This brings the service closer to local issues and needs, allows for drop-in surgeries as an additional way of raising awareness of mediation and further promotes volunteering. The satellites each have a staff member attached to them. Funding is provided for two of the satellites from South Yorkshire Police's Community Initiatives Programme, a third by SRB and the fourth by Sheffield City Council housing department.

Service provision

A non-typical neighbour mediation initiative: United Neighbours

A group of residents in Chelmsley Wood, Birmingham formed themselves into a scheme to help neighbours in dispute see each other's point of view. Calling themselves United Neighbours or UN, they offered a range of services depending on the dispute. These include individual advice and counselling over the phone. If the dispute is more serious, members of the team visit the neighbour and consider whether it would be worthwhile to visit the other neighbour involved.

Experience showed that joint meetings of both sides could help in resolving problems. Members of the team have gone on to develop different skills – some have taken mediation training, others have learnt British Sign Language or counselling skills. The scheme is considering becoming a community mediation service (Gowan, 2000, p. 32)

Comment: having developed into mediation through previous practice (rather than starting out with mediation), UN has the freedom that many a mediator has yearned for when dealing with a 'difficult' neighbour – the freedom to offer advice, information or individual counselling. This links to the definition of conciliation as explored in the section on 'Conciliation vs. mediation' in Chapter 1. However, most services would feel that the requirements of impartiality and not suggesting solutions would prevent any in-depth work with one client, even where mediation had proved to be unsuccessful.

4 Service users

Take-up of mediation by black and minority ethnic communities

Mediation UK's service profiles show that 73 per cent of member services monitor staff and volunteers by ethnicity. Unfortunately, the profiles do not reveal the results of this monitoring, so a national picture of mediators is hard to draw up. By and large, services' Annual Reports and the interviews we held with individual services showed that recruitment of black and minority ethnic mediators was in line with or below local minority population proportions. A contrary example is provided by Mediation in Kirklees: against a backdrop of 11 per cent of the community defining itself as coming from minority ethnic communities (1991 Census results), about 20 per cent of the service's volunteer mediators are from black and minority ethnic backgrounds.

Whereas 73 per cent of services ethnically monitor staff and mediators, only 58 per cent monitor their clients by ethnicity. Through its quality assurance mechanisms, Mediation UK has encouraged services to monitor this information. Services need to prove to themselves that they are accessible to all parts of their catchment community – and that they can demonstrate this accessibility to their funders and other supporters.

Services provided us with the following examples of their engagement with black and minority ethnic residents:

Service users

- *Dacorum*: the minority ethnic population in Dacorum is 2.5 per cent, but 5 per cent of service users are from a black and minority ethnic (BME) background. The service has a multi-language leaflet and has used an interpreter.

- *Luton*: the minority ethnic population of Luton was around 20 per cent according to the 1991 Census. Take-up monitoring in 2000 reflected these proportions fairly accurately, although some minority ethnic groups were marginally over-represented (e.g. Afro-Caribbeans, Chinese) while others were marginally under-represented (e.g. Indians and Pakistanis, although Bangladeshis were neither under- nor over-represented).

- *Kirklees*: about 80 per cent of the caseload involves people from BME backgrounds.

- *Newham Conflict and Change Project*: of 215 cases dealt with in 2000–01, 100 (47 per cent) were with white clients. The remaining 53 per cent were divided between various ethnic mixes, including 'unknown'.

- *Mediation Oxfordshire*: in terms of ethnicity, the service told us that it gets a roughly proportionate number of referrals (given the population) but has a somewhat poor record in getting these referrals to joint meetings. The service is currently doing a specific piece of outreach in East Oxford (which has the city's highest concentration of ethnic minority populations). The service's information leaflets have very recently been translated into the four main minority ethnic languages.

- *Cardiff Mediation*: resource constraints mean that the service cannot carry out continuous monitoring of take-up by audiences. Instead, it carries out periodic 'dip-stick' sampling to measure the parameters of age, gender, health/

disability, ethnicity and employment. The caseload does not mirror Cardiff's population, but rather the awareness of key referring agencies – some of which may be more aware of or more positive towards mediation than others.

Monitoring other than by ethnicity

Greenwich Mediation's Annual Report provided the most varied analysis of data. By age, 18 per cent of clients were between 16 and 25, 53 per cent were between 26 and 40, 21 per cent were between 41 and 60, and 8 per cent were over 60. Six per cent of clients reported a physical disability, 13 per cent a sensory disability and 1 per cent said that they were lesbian or gay. Employment status was also monitored: 62 per cent of service users were unemployed, 38 per cent employed.

As well as by ethnic background, Dacorum also monitors clients by age, type of housing and employment status. Generally, people from lower income backgrounds are involved in neighbour disputes – the two most deprived wards present many cases. The service has large numbers of older clients. It wonders if this is because older people tend to spend more time at home and are more susceptible to noticing disruption from neighbours.

It is not easy to determine the take-up of mediation by people of different socio-economic groups, as very few services carry out this level of monitoring. Research quoted in Mulcahy with Summerfield (2001, p. 55) suggests that people involved in neighbour disputes are more likely to be economically inactive and to have lower household incomes. Factors that account for this include the following:

- As shown in Chapter 3, 51 per cent of referrals come from local authority and social landlord housing officers, and lower socio-economic groups are more likely to be social housing tenants.

- The stresses imposed by living in a deprived community, coupled with higher density and more poorly constructed housing, are likely to provoke more community conflict
- Lower socio-economic groups have less access to conflict management and interpersonal development skills training.
- Social housing tenants may face pressure to go to mediation in order to ward off tenancy enforcement measures, whereas private tenants and owner-occupiers have a greater choice about whether to go to mediation.

Interestingly, research within the Mulcahy with Summerfield study of Southwark Mediation Centre (2001) shows that women are more likely to be parties in disputes referred to mediation, and that most disputes involved households of a single woman against another. Mulcahy with Summerfield suggest various possible reasons for this:

- Women are more likely to be economically inactive and thus more exposed to neighbours and problems within their immediate neighbourhood.
- Women may be more likely to be part of a dispute if it involves someone they are caring for.
- Women may be more willing to be referred to mediation, either because a constructive approach to problem-solving is more inherent to women, or because societal pressures constrain women from more violent expressions of anger and conflict.

Involving children in mediation

Most services encourage the participation of children if the children are perceived to be part of either the problem or the solution. Peer mediation has shown that primary school age children can be trained as mediators. Within neighbour disputes, services have shown that children can understand and take part constructively in mediation (the youngest example of a child participating in mediation that we came across was three years old), although mediators can often have difficulty in preventing the parents speaking on behalf of the child.

Services are aware of child protection issues, but some services are more willing to see children on their own (with parental consent), whereas others insist on the adults being present. If children are involved in a dispute mediated by Dacorum (e.g. mediation with school students), the service will adapt its procedure on a case-by-case basis and will always meet with the parents first.

For any service, if mediators are only available to visit during the day, then children at school will probably be excluded from meeting the mediators. If children are to be involved, then this is clearly not to the advantage of the mediation process.

Specific service comments on involving children

The training for Edinburgh's mediators focuses on strategies to get the child talking. Particular skills are needed for working with children: 'some otherwise proficient mediators can't help telling children what to do' (telephone interview with Edinburgh Community Mediation Service). Edinburgh commented that children intuitively like mediation as it is respectful and fair. Once separate from their parents, the child's story is more likely to emerge. The service reported one case where both children and parents in two households were arguing; the young women sorted out their issues, and the parents came and asked for mediation when they saw its success with their daughters.

UNITE, in Middlesbrough, sees no difference to a case when children are involved. Mediators encourage their participation early on and try and persuade them to come to the joint meeting.

For Leeds, the inclusion of children depends on the mediators. A joint meeting was described where children had their uninterrupted time along with the adults. It was a multi-party case, with 15 people attending the meeting along with four mediators. The dispute was partly about children's behaviour. Four children attended: one aged three, two aged six and seven, and a 14 year old. When the children had their chance to speak, one drew a picture of two enemies shaking hands.

5 Service Funders

Details of funding sources and levels

We came across a wide range of service incomes and income sources. Three main sources were identified: agency funding, charitable or community grant funding and self-generated income.

Agency funding

Virtually all services, whether in-house or independent, relied on some form of local authority funding. Housing departments, social services and environmental health departments were the main identified funders.

Other agency funders included housing associations, police, Community Safety Partnerships and health authorities. Agency income is either in the form of annual block grants, or purchase of mediation on a case-by-case basis.

Agency grants ranged in size from the £550 from Elmbridge Borough Council, to the £145,518 raised by Southwark Mediation Centre (1997–98) from Borough, City and County Councils. Typical funding awards listed in the service Annual Reports that we examined ranged from £30,000 to £60,000.

For services that charged on a case-by-case basis, the following are sample figures.

Mediation Works charges referral agencies between £300 and £400 per case. Its Best Value report cites the following further evidence of cost-effectiveness:

- An average cost of between £162 and £429 (Crowe, Neighbour Disputes Responses by Social Landlords, Chartered Institute of Housing, July 1999), compared to an estimated £3,908 in legal costs of a contested possession order.

- Birmingham City Council's in-house mediation service estimates that the cost of mediating an agreement is, on average, 10 per cent of the cost of obtaining a contested possession order.

- This compares to Southwark Mediation Centre's unit case cost of £410.48. Of this, £225.79 relates to specific case tasks, but the cost rises to £410.48 with the inclusion of general mediator tasks (supervision, office tasks, etc.) and overall organisational costs (Mulcahy with Summerfield, 2000).

- The Annual Report of SEAMS mediation service (covering Braintree, Bury St Edmunds and Colchester) gives an average cost of £300 per case.

- Mediation in Action averages a charge of £550 per case, based on fixed fees per visit and joint meeting.

Charitable or government community grants

The National Lottery Charities Board (now the Community Fund), Single Regeneration Budget, Health and Education Action Zones and the new Community Regeneration grants have provided significant sums to mediation services over recent years. UNITE in Middlesbrough, for example, was awarded Lottery funding of £250,000 over five years. Smaller services often also access local and national charities (examples include the Tudor Trust, Allen Lane Foundation, Sir James Reckitt Foundation and Lloyds TSB).

Self-generated funds

These arose primarily out of training fees to external agencies, as well as consultancy and conflict resolution work in organisations. In services' Annual Reports for 2000–01, typical examples are Bliss (Blyth Valley, Northumberland): £10,797; Greenwich Mediation: £11,786; and Wolverhampton Mediation: £9,739 (this sum includes income from delivering a professional development certificate in mediation through a partnership with a local college).

For services that have the confidence and can develop the opportunities to market themselves in this way, self-generated funds can clearly provide a significant funding opportunity.

Oxfordshire Mediation invites self-referrers to make a voluntary contribution and offers some basic information on the direct costs of providing mediation. A small amount of money is raised this way and is an interesting challenge to the perception that a voluntary sector community mediation service cannot raise funds directly from service users.

A comparison of two services

This comparison is intended to reflect the difference in scale of provision of two independent (i.e. not local authority managed) services. Not all services look towards expansion as automatically desirable or necessary.

Elmbridge Independent Mediation Service
Income year to March 2001: £3,623 from three principal sources – Elmbridge Housing Trust (£2,000), Surrey Police (£600) and Elmbridge Borough Council (£550) (figures from the service's Annual Report to 31 March 2001). Funding has been agreed for 2001–02 to a total of £4,400.

Service funders

> **Newham Conflict and Change Programme**
> Income in 2000/01: £233,378. Of this, £192,297 came from grants and 'other' (including income-generation activities) totalled £41,081.

Private income for mediation services

We found no example of a community mediation service that charged its service users, although Face to Face Mediation (Herefordshire) is just establishing itself as a service aimed specifically at taking referrals of neighbour disputes from local solicitors. As the service has just begun, it is too early to evaluate the success of encouraging these private clients to pay for mediation – nor how frequently legally aided clients will be funded to try mediation during the lifetime of the dispute.

The fact that no community mediation service so far has on any significant scale charged the parties for neighbour mediation partly arises from an assumption within the sector that mediation should be free at the point of use. There is also a sense that, while for family mediation the situation (i.e. the divorce or separation) has arisen from choices that the parties have previously made, in the main it is well-nigh impossible to choose one's neighbours. This is particularly true for social housing tenants on waiting lists, who are limited in the number of offers of housing that they can refuse without penalty. However, owner-occupiers can rarely conduct satisfactory investigations into their potential neighbours and disputes can arise after people have been neighbours for several years.

Pragmatically, however, there is great difficulty in raising private fee income from service users when significant proportions of neighbour disputes arise in economically deprived areas.

This has effectively restricted the vast majority of neighbour mediation to voluntary or statutory sector organisations and commercially based, fee-charging services for neighbour disputes are extremely rare. We could only find two: Face to Face (Herefordshire) and Mediation in Action.

> ### Mediation in Action: a private neighbour mediation service
>
> A private partnership has for five years been providing neighbour mediation services in the Thames Valley. Individual service level agreements with a range of agencies (councils, housing associations, environmental health departments and the police) provide about 100 cases a year, at an average cost of £550 per case. Mediation thus remains free at the point of use – and only agency referrals are accepted, not self-referrals. The mediators act initially as an assessment service (see Chapter 3, section on 'Pre-mediation activities') and find that this contact with both sides then makes it easier to move into a more traditional mediation-type role to help resolve the dispute.
>
> Working within the Thames Valley means that the two-mediator partnership inevitably provides neighbour mediation to populations that are also covered by other voluntary or statutory mediation services. This does produce competition, with Mediation in Action demonstrating that some statutory agencies prefer to purchase mediation when needed rather than pay to support the ongoing existence of a local charitable or in-house mediation service.

But, whereas the difficulty of making neighbour mediation viable as a private commercial exercise has meant that neighbour mediation services by and large do not face competition with commercial mediators, family mediation services increasingly find themselves competing with solicitor-mediators who provide family mediation funded by legal aid.

This lack of competition for neighbour mediation was threatened at one point. In 1997, the Legal Aid Board funded mediation as a disbursement within a neighbour dispute case, but, despite an expectation that this precedent would prove to be an opening of the floodgates, funding restrictions meant that this was not repeated in other similar cases. Had this not been the case, the neighbour mediation field might now look very different. It is possible to imagine that, had private or legal aid funding become significant income streams for services, the resulting link between mediation and litigated civil disputes would have led to an increasing partnership with the Lord Chancellor's Department and the county courts. In time, the UK might have generated an American-type model of mediation services allied to local courts, where cases are routinely diverted to in-house or resident mediators and the court itself becomes a fallback should mediation not produce a resolution.

This is still a possible development for community mediation services, but involvement of legally trained mediators within the Central London County Court pilot (see Chapter 1, section on 'Mapping of other forms of mediation') has ensured that litigation of civil disputes is likely to remain beyond the reach of community mediation services for some time to come.

In recent correspondence we have seen between the Lord Chancellor's Department and a solicitor and community mediator, it is clear that the Government still sees legally aided mediation primarily as a service that solicitors can access for their clients (as a disbursement of fees, similar to obtaining an expert's report in a personal injury case), rather than by funding services directly and thus avoiding the need to go to a solicitor in the first place. Direct contracts under the Community Legal Service, such as those already existing for family mediation services, are *not* envisaged for community mediation services; and the only services that will be eligible to provide mediation via a legal aid certificate will be Quality Marked services using accredited or 'competent' mediators. We look further at the Quality Mark in Chapter 6.

Service sustainability

We have already identified that many services face difficulties in securing their financial future. Hughes and Waddington (2001) identify key features of sustainability as demonstrated by UK community mediation services:

- well-established community organisations
- adequate and flexible funding from a range of sources
- expansion to deliver a multi-mediation service over wide geographical areas
- a high profile and good links with an established community network
- provision of quality assurance and 'best value'
- ability to demonstrate their benefits through monitoring and evaluation
- researched and piloted schemes that demonstrated good practice.

In contrast, the research identifies organisational capacity, lack of funding, lack of meaningful partnerships, poor public relations and local accountability as significant barriers to development. Successful projects had redefined or repackaged themselves, diversified services, aligned them to national strategies and put more resources into public relations.

Many of the mechanisms identified can also be used to generate service growth as well as ensure longer-term survival. Tony Billinghurst, Director of Mediation UK, actively encourages service diversification as a means to attain sustainability and confirmed to us his view that services have encountered practical obstacles to diversification (securing funding, establishing partnerships), rather than being opposed to the idea in principle.

Services have a key role to play in capacity-building within local communities, as Hughes and Waddington (2001) demonstrate. Not only does capacity-building offer longer-term preventive strategies against violent conflict, it also offers an alternative route for service sustainability.

A model of capacity-building has emerged from a feasibility study for the creation of Rhondda Cynon Taf mediation service. The study found that local residents were not interested in using mediation or becoming a mediator, but they were interested in addressing the conflicts and problems that they faced in their local community.

Rhondda Cynon Taf has therefore developed a model enabling a continuum of local resident involvement in conflict and mediation. Starting with training in conflict awareness and conflict management skills, residents could move on to do grassroots community work/liaison, and could then choose to train as independent mediators working within their own community. A local mediation service could provide a way of getting mediation experience and skills relevant for other work, which could lead to employment in either the mediation field or another sector – or lead to income generation for the service itself. Quality for individual mediators would be provided through individual support and supervision by their nearest service – and that service being tied into quality and competence via its membership of Mediation UK.

Local authority support and funding

Liebmann (1998) lists five reasons why local authorities might be interested in supporting (and therefore funding) neighbour mediation:

1. the failure of legal remedies to deal with neighbour conflict
2. a desire to provide an alternative to existing methods of resolving disputes
3. a belief that mediation is more appropriate for certain types of disputes
4. the realisation that mediation has a real potential for rebuilding communities
5. a sense that mediation may be more cost-effective and take less time than traditional methods.

Recent developments provide three additions to this list:

1. The Crime and Disorder Act 1998 (which introduced Anti-social Behaviour Orders, or ASBOs), the additional powers to evict under the 1996 Housing Act and the higher media profile on neighbour disputes through such programme as *Neighbours from Hell* and *Neighbours at War* have raised expectations of tenants towards social landlords to deal more immediately and more effectively with neighbour problems.
2. The Home Office Guidance Notes on ASBOs provide that mediation should at least have been considered before an application for an ASBO is made (para. 3.13). So, local authorities without access to mediation risk ASBO

applications being refused because they have been unable to try other alternatives first. And authorities with access to mediation need to write mediation into protocols on dealing with neighbour nuisance so that mediation is considered (and can be shown to have been considered) during their handling of disputes.

3   Performance indicators put local authority services under the spotlight. Even a performance indicator such as 'satisfaction with housing services' has relevance to the need to have effective responses to tenants' complaints about their neighbours. If one tenant complains about their neighbour and the complaint is not resolved, the original tenant may then make a complaint against their housing officer for failing to resolve the situation, leading to a perception of ineffectiveness or dissatisfaction by the tenant towards the local authority.

The result is that, of the Annual Reports we received, virtually all services list local authority funding among their sources of income. But local authority funding comes with a price.

Mediation services and the dilemma of social landlord funding

All local authority areas contain different types of housing tenure – local authority tenants, housing association and other social landlord tenants, and private tenants and owner-occupiers. Neighbour disputes result in many agencies potentially being involved, from landlords and local authority environmental health departments to agencies such as the police, solicitors, community safety partnerships, local councillors and voluntary support agencies. Because no one agency or landlord has sole responsibility for responding to *all* neighbour disputes, there is no agency who is thus primarily interested in mediation being available to all local residents.

This gap produces difficulties for services in seeking funding, and those difficulties are experienced by Mediation UK on a national level (see section on 'Does mediation work? The cost-effectiveness of mediation' later in this chapter).

So far as local services are concerned, Mediation UK encourages the broadest possible access to mediation by the public. Narrowly restricted funding can, however, limit access; and the principal source of local authority funding – housing departments' Housing Revenue Account – can legally only be spent on council tenants. Services that are legally wholly funded by Housing Revenue Account can legally only mediate disputes that involve council tenants.

The natural temptation for a local service is then to seek General Fund funding from elsewhere within the Council – typically, from environmental services, community safety, or social services departments. As the locally raised element of the General Fund comes primarily from Council Tax, local authority tenants who have access to a service funded by both the General Fund (Council Tax) and Housing Revenue Account (tenants' rents) can legitimately argue that they are paying for the service twice.

Further complications come when a service attracts funding from a local housing association. If the service wishes to be accessible by the whole community, the moment one local housing association part-funds a mediation service, the service must decide whether it should refuse cases from other housing association tenants unless that association also contributes to the service's funding (either by grant or on a case-by-case basis).

These funding dilemmas often result from a service's attempts to broaden either its funding or client base, and the dilemmas are widespread within the neighbour mediation field. To promote accessibility, services can insist that any service level agreement with a local authority guarantees access by all residents regardless of tenure. At the same time, the service should make clear that where the authority funds that service from is up to the authority to manage. If the local authority is determined enough to buy mediation then the service can win the game; but an anxious time of bluff and counter-bluff may well be engaged in first, especially if employees within the service are dependent on the outcome of the negotiations.

The impact of Best Value

As a successor to Compulsory Competitive Tendering, Best Value is forcing local authorities to review all services on a rolling five-year programme to ensure both quality and value for money. In-house mediation services are of course directly affected by Best Value reviews. But independent services that receive local authority funding are also affected, as they will need to demonstrate that they are a cost-effective provision that the authority should continue to subsidise.

A report by Mediation Works (Monmouthshire's independent mediation service) entitled *A Report on Mediation as a Best Value Approach to Neighbour Nuisance and Anti-social Behaviour in Social Housing* identifies mediation as a cost-effective alternative to local authority enforcement procedures. However, an emphasis within the study on comparing mediation with the costs of contested possession hearings is not wholly helpful, as of course not all of neighbour nuisance cases end up in court.

But this highlights a more fundamental difficulty in proving cost-effectiveness: even if the dispute is resolved, it is impossible to know for certain whether the dispute might have resolved itself anyway – or whether the resolution has indeed avoided lengthy enforcement activity by the landlord.

Does mediation work? The cost-effectiveness of mediation

Rightly, this question is one that neighbour mediation services are regularly asked. Clients want to know if the process they are committing to has some hope of resolving the dispute; the media look for overall success rates to go alongside case studies and interviews with service users; and funders want to know that they are getting value for money.

The first response to this question must come in the form of Mediation UK's Annual Survey, which asks services to evaluate outcomes according to the categories shown in Table 3.

Table 3 Mediation UK's Annual Survey

Category	Per cent
Agreement on all issues	19
Partial agreement on all issues	11
No agreement but improved communication	13
Assistance to one party	7
Dispute resolved without intervention	5
Mediation felt to be inappropriate	8
Closure following withdrawal	23
Closure because of differences	5
Closure for other reason	6
No response from either party	10

Source: Mediation UK's Annual Community Mediation Dispute Survey 2001.

So, on a national basis, the proportion of cases that achieved full or partial agreement on all issues (the first two categories) is 30 per cent.

At first sight, this 30 per cent success could be considered low, given that mediation is expressly about enabling the parties to reach an agreement. The extent to which that 30 per cent can be seen to be a good success rate depends on how the following factors are rated:

Service funders

- A neighbour dispute is an irrational and swift-moving process; by contrast, mediation is a rational, staged and explicitly cognitive process.

- The parties have already demonstrated themselves to be unable or unwilling to resolve the problem on their own, and mediation keeps the responsibility on the parties themselves to generate and agree solutions.

- Given the probable state of the dispute, any move forward is a gain (including improved communication or understanding about the situation).

Moreover, success depends on one's point of view. For neighbours, success is usually judged by the effectiveness of the process in resolving the dispute, although other outcomes (renewal of relationship or clearing up of misunderstandings) can be equally valuable; whereas, for housing officers, a case is successfully referred to mediation if the housing officer then hears no more from either side – regardless of whether the dispute was actually resolved.

In the most significant research into the financial benefits of neighbour mediation (Dignan *et al.*, 1996), mediation is shown to be a fairly resource-intensive response to neighbour nuisance – especially when compared to the significant amount of low-level informal interventions carried out by housing officers and environmental health officers. Comparison of these two types of intervention are hard to establish. This is because of key differences to disputes adopted by the two approaches:

- the non-judgemental approach of mediation compared to the more adversarial approaches of social landlords

- landlords' concern with procedural safeguards rather than mediation's more flexible approach to dealing with the conflict
- mediation's emphasis on encouraging the parties to take responsibility for settling the dispute, rather than submitting the dispute to investigation and adjudication by a housing officer or other external person.

Dignan et al.'s research does identify 'a reasonably fair and reliable method' (Liebmann, 1998, p. 240) of comparing the costs of mediation and other agency mechanisms of dealing with neighbour disputes. The method could be used to compare on both a global and unit cost basis, and would enable comparisons to be made both of the effort made by the agency to resolve the dispute (whether by mediation or by other more traditional remedies) and the quality of outcomes.

Dignan et al.'s study was limited by not including 'quality of outcomes' research (as there were no interviews with neighbours who had used mediation as well as other agency methods of neighbour dispute resolution). The research therefore concludes that an effective procedure for evaluating quality of outcomes still needs to be developed; but, when this became available, it would then be straightforward to produce a mechanism to accurately judge the value for money of mediation in relation to other resolution methods.

Implementation of this further comparative quality outcome evaluation is now being planned by Dignan, by comparing two areas with and without a local mediation service. York has been identified as a community with access to neighbour mediation and an equivalent area without access to mediation (using the Chartered Institute of Public Finance and Accountancy's local authority comparisons) is now being sought.

National government funding – England

We outlined above the difficulties that mediation services have experienced in raising local authority funding which arise principally because no one local authority department has sole responsibility for ensuring the presence of a neighbour mediation service. At a national level, government funding for Mediation UK faces a similar difficulty.

Central government has acknowledged that Mediation UK does meet the interests of different government departments, but this acknowledgement has not gone further than joint departmental funding of Mediation UK. Coordinated by the Home Office Active Community Unit, four departments provide funding for Mediation UK: the Department of Health, the Lord Chancellor's Department, the Home Office and the Department of Transport, Local Government and the Regions (DTLR). The funding totals £120,000 for 2002–03. Ironically, the Active Community Unit's role is to support and encourage volunteering – a further example of mediation having to find a niche within which to stand, rather than stepping into a clearly defined place among national government activities. Mediation was described to us by the Active Community Unit as being valued across government as a *function* rather than a *policy* priority.

The Alternative Dispute Resolution (ADR) Unit in the Lord Chancellor's Department is another demonstration of mediation 'falling between stools'. Mediation is a form of ADR; but, as the primary focus of the ADR Unit is commercial mediation (i.e. the mediation of litigated disputes) and, as the cases that community mediation deals with are not usually likely to go to court, community mediation is not a priority within the Unit.

National government funding – Scotland and Wales

The devolution of power to the Welsh Assembly and the Scottish Executive has provided the opportunity for government funding within a relatively small group of mediation services. As such, the link between government and individual service provision is much closer than is experienced in England.

Wales

There are six neighbour mediation services in Wales (out of eight community mediation services in total). Individual services are funded in very similar ways to English services, although some services receive direct funding from the Welsh Assembly (over the last three years, £94,000 of National Assembly funding has gone directly to Welsh community mediation services, including a £75,000 grant from the Sustainable Communities Fund in Wales shared between five services).

Mediation was initially supported by the Housing Division of the Welsh Assembly, but is now likely to come under the Community Regeneration and Social Inclusion Unit in the near future. This Unit is to likely to be approached by Mediation Wales for funding when the present lottery grant expires in 2002.

Mediation Wales, a branch of Mediation UK, was set up with National Lottery Charities Board funding in 1999 – £180,000 over three years. Helen Prior, the current Director of Mediation Wales, reported that the Welsh Assembly as a devolved institution had opportunities for comparatively closer links with Mediation Wales (as a similar devolved organisation from Mediation UK) than Mediation UK had with Westminster government departments. Similarly, the smaller number of services in Wales enables a much closer link between Mediation Wales and members services than can exist between Mediation UK and English and Scottish services.

Service funders

Scotland

Scotland has nine neighbour mediation services, out of 13 community mediation services in total. Glasgow remains the principal populous area without a local mediation service. (National media incorrectly reported recently that a mediator had been appointed following the murder of a refugee housed on a Glasgow housing estate, but in fact the person appointed was to coordinate the Council's response to asylum seekers.)

To date an organisation called SACRO, which also manages five of the Scottish community mediation services, has been the principal channel for Scottish Executive funding of the community mediation sector. The Scottish Executive promotes the systematic development of mediation within Scotland; one SACRO post funded by the Executive is specifically designed to support local authorities in the local development of mediation. A series of booklets and briefing papers is being produced to cover areas such as good practice, choosing a model of service delivery, and monitoring and evaluation. In an example which their English counterparts would do well to follow, Members of the Scottish Parliament invited Edinburgh Community Mediation Service to offer guidance to MSPs on positive ways of dealing with conflict!

There is further liaison between the Executive and local authorities via a Neighbourhood Officer, whose role is to support practice and policy on a range of services addressing anti-social behaviour. An active Scottish Mediation Network provides a focus for inter-service communication, support and sharing of best practice. The Network is made up of a variety of mediation strands – neighbour, victim–offender, family, environmental and special educational needs mediation.

A three-year grant of £210,000 has just been awarded to Mediation UK to open an office and provide coordination for the Scottish Mediation Network. Awarded by the Community Fund

(Scotland), this money is a welcome and significant contribution to the Scottish mediation sector.

6 Quality standards

Major developments for mediation quality standards were taking place as this report was being written. This chapter therefore sets out a brief history of quality standards within the community mediation field, introduces the Community Legal Service's new Quality Mark and examines a simple quality system designed by a small mediation service to meet its own particular requirements.

A brief history of mediation standard-setting

Mediation UK has been the primary mover on developing mediation quality standards in the community mediation field. Mediation UK's Strategic Plan 1997–2000 put delivery of quality at the heart of its mission ('to ensure everyone has access to quality mediation services in their local communities' and an accompanying strategic aim to 'ensure the highest possible standard of mediation'). The need for sustainability has led to a parallel and less exalted reason within individual services in their search for quality – namely, the ability to demonstrate quality gives more chance to attract funding.

Mediation UK's earliest most significant publication on quality, drawn from the experience of its predecessor organisation FIRM (Forum for Initiatives in Reparation and Mediation), was the Mediation UK *Practice Standards* (1993, revised 1998). An Accreditation Committee, established in 1993 and drawn from Mediation UK's membership, was charged with promoting the application of those standards. Accreditation was seen to be relevant in four areas: the accreditation of *services*, of *mediators*, of *training courses* and of *trainers*. Of these, accreditation of trainers is the only area in which significant progress has not been made.

Quality systems

The codification of quality service provision in the voluntary and statutory sectors has been influenced in recent years by the following:

- funders have increased accountability requirements imposed on funded organisations by now linking funding to service delivery targets, outputs and evidence of effectiveness within the community

- a corresponding proliferation of quality standards, some of which are used as benchmarks by funders and government and thus are written into organisational development plans

- competition for funding, where services which can quantifiably justify their effectiveness stand a better chance of securing funding

- government promotion of continuing adult education and qualifications through skills-based learning (National Vocational Qualifications).

One of the risks of quality systems is that, in striving to demonstrate the quality, they can interfere with actually providing that quality. This can happen if a quality system has too onerous administrative requirements, or if an organisation (while in reality providing quality service) has too much to do to document and codify its practice. In either case, resources devoted to providing the service are diverted to satisfying the demands of the quality system; and specific requirements may be satisfied on paper without producing a concurrent improvement in service provision.

Quality systems and the community mediation field

These dilemmas about quality systems have in part influenced resistance to Mediation UK's mechanisms for the accreditation of services and mediators. This resistance has come both from some member services and from individual members.

For individuals, a religious or personal desire to promote mediation has led to their involvement in Mediation UK and its predecessor FIRM. This value-based commitment to conflict resolution sits uneasily with attempts to justify mediation on financial or target-based terms. This unease has been exacerbated as Mediation UK has moved in recent years from principally supporting individual members to prioritising its support for and promotion of its service members.

Of more fundamental implication is the opposition that some long-established services have had to accreditation on the basis that, abruptly stated: 'we know we deliver quality mediation and we don't need to prove it to anyone'. Having described it to us as the 'horror of accreditation', many services now recognise the need to be able to justify – or at least demonstrate – the quality service they provide. An influx of local authority managed services has further tipped the balance of Mediation UK membership in favour of standard-setting and monitoring. This recognition has not, however, translated automatically into enthusiastic support of Mediation UK's sponsored quality systems.

With that context in mind, we now turn to a brief examination of Mediation UK's work in promoting the accreditation of services, mediators and training courses.

Accreditation of services

An accreditation pack was produced to structure Mediation UK's recognition of services which achieved the quality of service set out in the *Practice Standards*. Piloted in 1994–96, the accreditation of services slowly took off; there developed a process of service application, scrutiny of documentation, and a day-long visit by a team of two Mediation UK assessors who submitted a report and recommendation to the Accreditation Committee for decision. By April 2001, 15 accredited services were listed in Mediation UK's list of neighbour mediation services, with a number of services either midway through or committed to starting the accreditation process.

These 15 services represent just over 10 per cent of Mediation UK's neighbour mediation service membership and that percentage is a reflection of the difficulties that Mediation UK experienced in encouraging member services to apply for accreditation. As well as the 'horror' of accreditation, Mediation UK's justifiable decision to charge services that applied for accreditation (at a subsidised rate), together with more or less accurately understood concerns about the difficulty and labour-intensiveness involved in preparing a service for accreditation, all contributed to this low take-up.

Mediation UK's accreditation system for community mediation services in England and Wales came to an abrupt end in the spring of 2001 with the planned introduction of the Community Legal Service's Quality Mark for mediation services.

The Legal Services Commission (which has replaced the Legal Aid Board) launched the Community Legal Service (CLS) in April 2000, and to support the CLS a set of quality standards was developed for three different levels of legal service provision: Information, General Help and Specialist Help. From the outset, the CLS made clear that funding and local partnership opportunities would flow from service providers that could meet these quality standards and that were thus awarded the newly introduced Quality Mark.

Perceiving that community mediation falls outside the three categories of Information, General Help and Specialist Help (which refers particularly to legal representation), Mediation UK successfully lobbied for a further Quality Mark (QM) standard to be introduced for community mediation services. A draft QM standard has been produced and the Quality Mark is due to be introduced in June 2002. Mediation services will be able to apply for the Quality Mark, be audited by the CLS and thus gain national recognition of their service provision.

Two things are important to note about the Mediation QM Standard. The first is that the standard was written by a working group that included representatives from Mediation UK and the UK College of Family Mediators. As such, it closely reflects both the management standards within the Family Mediation Pilot Project Quality Assurance Standard and Mediation UK's Practice Standards for community mediation services. As a positive development, therefore, this government-endorsed standard for mediation services (including community mediation) matches Mediation UK's own preferences for how the quality of mediation can be assessed. The standard is 'a milestone in the creation of a nationally recognised quality standard for alternative dispute resolution and legal services' (from the Foreword to the Mediation QM Standard consultation paper). That Mediation UK has been involved in this process, and that alternative dispute resolution is set alongside legal representation within the CLS, demonstrates that community mediation has taken a significant step in being mainstreamed into government thinking on resolving conflict within the community.

Second, and less agreeably, the proposed introduction of the Mediation QM sounded the immediate death knell of Mediation

UK's service accreditation programme in England and Wales (the accreditation programme, which is not covered by the Community Legal Service, remains available for the 13 community mediation services in Scotland). Not only was the QM a nationally recognised audit process specifically targeted at community (and family) mediation services – and thus had a far higher profile and credibility than Mediation UK's own accreditation programme – but also, application for the QM is free to services, whereas Mediation UK charged services in order to cover the accreditation programme's costs. In March 2001, the accreditation programme was halted; services thinking of applying for accreditation were advised to wait for the start of the CLS QM; and already accredited services would be passported automatically into the new QM.

We came across opposition to the Quality Mark during our research for this review. The Development Coordinator of one service, South Worcestershire, characterised the QM as 'a threat to volunteering' on the basis that the requirements of the QM (mechanistic, standards-driven, judgemental) are fundamentally at odds with the ethos of volunteering (people-centred, needs driven, generosity).

Oxfordshire Mediation acknowledged the QM to be a mechanism for raising standards, but mentioned concern that it also risks significantly increasing core costs (greater supervision frequency, file review, hours open to the public, increased documentation and case administration).

Time will show whether the QM will become widely embraced within the neighbour mediation field.

Accreditation of mediators

Mediation UK's desire has been to enable mediators from individual services to achieve national acknowledgement of their skills. At the same time, there has been clear recognition of the broad backgrounds from which those mediators come, as services successfully encourage people from all walks of life to become mediators. Mediation UK's focus has therefore been on producing a national qualification based primarily on experience and observed practice rather than on academic standards.

National Vocational Qualifications (NVQs) were chosen as providing the most accessible qualification that was also rigorous and involved an element of external assessment (to ensure consistent quality across the awards). Standards were devised to cover neighbour, victim–offender and peer mediation. Once the NVQ was available to services, Mediation UK also put in place a process of accreditation, whereby attainment of the NVQ in mediation was a major step to becoming a Mediation UK accredited mediator.

Unhappily, take-up of the NVQ has been extremely low, primarily because of the intensive nature of preparing a portfolio and the costs involved for both internal and external verification of the award.

The Quality Mark has introduced an alternative means of attaining national acknowledgement of a mediator's skills. Requirement D5 of the Mediation Quality Mark Standard requires a minimum number of 'competent mediators' within each Quality Marked service.

Mediation UK is the body responsible for ensuring assessment of competence of mediators. Requirement D5.2 sets out the following percentages of competent mediators that services applying for the Quality Mark must attain:

- 25 per cent of mediators must be assessed as competent prior to the pre-Quality Mark audit
- 50 per cent within a year after the pre-Quality Mark audit

- 75 per cent within two years after the pre-Quality Mark audit.

To allow for change of mediator personnel – and for mediators who choose not to apply for competence – the service is not required at any point to have more than 75 per cent of its mediators assessed as competent.

These are significant standards to reach. Through a Quality Practice Group, Mediation UK is in the process of designing an assessment of competence that individual services can operate. The emphasis has been on ensuring that the process is straightforward, that it requires as little collation of evidence by mediators as possible and that prior experience is placed at a premium (to remove the need for further training of already experienced mediators). The assessment process has been drafted but not finalised at the time of writing this report; Mediation UK's agreement with the Community Legal Service is that the CLS will not enquire into the details of the competency process, leaving it up to Mediation UK to design and implement the quality process it feels best suits the needs of its services.

Accreditation of training courses

The third developed area of accreditation has been work by Mediation UK on an accredited training course. In 1996, the National Open College Network (NOCN) gave its endorsement to Mediation UK's Training Programme for Community Mediation Skills. This endorsement opened the way for Department of Education and Employment funding through local Open College Network colleges.

The paperwork involved in satisfactory completion of a NOCN mediation course, together with the technical structure of learning outcomes (off-putting to people not familiar with modern adult education methods), has limited the number of services that offer the accredited training course. A further handicap has been the fact that completion of the course was not enough to guarantee becoming an accredited mediator – further evidenced practice was also required. This removed the incentive for services to offer the course to mediators who were seeking a mediation qualification.

The five-year NOCN validation expired in 2001 and the NOCN course has been rewritten and relaunched, along with a Mediation UK support package. The intention within that rewriting was to simplify the course to make it more user-friendly. The emphasis has shifted from accrediting a training course to accrediting the competencies that mediators are required to show in their practice.

Discussions are also taking place within Mediation UK (unresolved at the time of writing) as to whether satisfactory completion of the course will be sufficient to guarantee competence within the Quality Mark for newly trained mediators. If this can be agreed, it will offer a significant incentive for mediation services to run the accredited course, as it will enormously simplify the service's attainment of the annual percentage targets of competent mediators.

Summary of accreditation and Quality Mark standards

The next few years will reveal the level of take-up of the Quality Mark and the new accredited training course, and will thus reflect the extent to which community mediation services have moved towards embracing external standards. Simplification of both training courses and assessment of mediator competence will hopefully encourage wider take-up of these Mediation UK supported quality systems.

Innovative services are already identifying the funding opportunities within the new systems. UNITE (in Middlesbrough), for example, has already registered as an accredited centre for delivery of the Open College Network mediation training course and intends to become an assessment centre for the NVQ.

During this review, profound opposition to the Quality Mark was expressed. It tends to come under one of two heads. The first is concern about the time and resource commitment that applying for the Quality Mark is believed to involve and that there is no guarantee of funded work arising as a result. The second is a more value-based resistance, claiming that service delivery does not always improve through such quality measures and that they risk stifling service innovation and creativity.

A different approach to ensuring quality service provision

Waverley Community Mediation Service (WCMS) has introduced its own simple quality system focused on the resources of the service and the needs of its referral agencies and mediators. Some mediators as volunteers in other organisations had bad experiences of being the subject of quality systems and were wary of similar burdens being imposed by WCMS. The service was also keen to find a quality system that was appropriate to the size of the service and the resources available within it. So it raised two questions:

1 What will develop quality within the service?

2 How do we need to measure our mediating in order to be sure that we are delivering a quality service?

The answer to the first question, based on the learning culture within the organisation, was that quality will grow primarily by encouraging 'a culture of self-appraisal and personal development arising from case experience' (WCMS Quality Assurance Policy). This is supported by an attitude of encouraging people to get things right and not to penalise for things done wrong but to use mistakes as an opportunity to learn. Peer feedback and debriefing, observed practice once a year, regular mediators' meetings, individual supervision and observation of face-to-face meetings complement the mediators being responsible for promoting their own professional development.

As for the second question, after long thought, the service decided that evaluation of service delivery and outcomes is best done by the funding and referral agencies, rather than by the parties themselves. It felt that clients' expectations about service delivery tend to go no further than whether or not the dispute is resolved and, in any event, the parties are not knowledgeable enough about mediation to judge how the mediators have managed the process and how well they have conducted themselves as mediators. The service therefore meets regularly with its funding and referral agencies to discuss case outcomes and service delivery; there is of course also a complaints procedure should clients be unhappy with the service they have received.

In conjunction with the service's documented procedures and the learning culture within the organisation, the Quality Assurance Policy is summarised on two sides of A4 (including target response times to referrals and enquiries).

The service indicated to us that it would only consider going for the Quality Mark should a new funder require it. Even then, the service may consider that the work involved in going for the Quality Mark may not be justified by the additional work and funding that would result.

7 Future trends and tensions

We conclude this review of community mediation by looking at some of the opportunities and tensions that the sector is likely to face over the next few years.

Service sustainability and capacity-building

Neighbour mediation is generally acknowledged to be an important part of an agency's response to community disorder and conflict. However, while it may be a necessary option of intervention, it is rarely seen as glamorous work. Thus some services, having successfully sought diversification beyond neighbour mediation in order to broaden their funding base and thereby ensure service sustainability, still often find that the core work of the service – i.e. mediating neighbour disputes – remains under-funded and is subsidised by other income streams.

Mediation services' strength is often their integrity of practice and responsibilities towards clients and referrers. This can sometimes become too rigid (e.g. over-stressing of confidentiality when reporting back to referral agencies, or an inflexible approach to supporting clients if mediation is not appropriate). Nevertheless, services get respect from funders for their impartiality and integrity, and have taken advantage of it to great effect (as the section on 'Other forms of neigbourhood-based mediation' in Chapter 3 of this review shows.)

Future trends and tensions

The route ahead is certain to include larger mediation services that provide a multiplicity of mediation-type interventions (sometimes referred to as multi-mediation services). Such services may well become the equivalent of a one-stop conflict resolution centre, providing mediation, conciliation, facilitation and other imaginative interventions within a whole range of community conflicts. Some links between family and community mediation – Shropshire Mediation Services and Mediation Advisory Services (Stafford) – are examples of combined family and community mediation services.

Large-scale government funding initiatives, such as SRB, Community Regeneration (targeted at the 88 most deprived English local authority districts) and the opportunities provided by Local Strategic Partnerships, all offer ways in which community capacity-building could become part of a mediation service's work.

Engagement in violent conflict

We have demonstrated that services have been willing to engage in addressing the roots of violent community conflict (LEAP, Southwark Mediation Centre; see section on 'An analysis of traditional neighbour mediation cases' in Chapter 3). The desperate need for an effective tool to respond to such conflicts creates a tremendous opportunity for mediation services to deepen their involvement in community conflict issues.

Mediation UK and victim–offender mediation

Although not strictly within the brief of this review, one definite trend arising from the 1998 Crime and Disorder Act has been the mainstreaming of the provision of mediation and reparation into the youth criminal justice system. This mainstreaming has been echoed by some parts of the National Probation Service limiting its funding for traditional adult victim–offender mediation. Mediation UK may well find itself needing to adjust and reappraise its role in supporting and promoting victim–offender mediation under its broad 'community mediation' umbrella.

The impact of the Quality Mark

As explored in Chapter 6 of this review, the level of take-up of the new Quality Mark by services will reflect Mediation UK's success in encouraging services to address quality standards.

Payment of mediators

The increasing use of paid mediators will force a confrontation between services that see payment as a pragmatic step forward and those that see volunteering as the key element of an effective neighbour mediation process. Services that pay their mediators will continue to grow in number regardless of appeals to what are perceived to be fundamental mediation principles, but the conflict will provide a further stage in Mediation UK's development from its grassroots origins, and may well provoke a positive exploration of the values of mediation and how they are effectively put into practice.

Academic criticism

Although an academic analysis of the theoretical basis of mediation was not within the remit of this review, predominantly left-wing academic criticism of mediation does point to some fundamental tensions within the mediation of neighbour disputes. Four criticisms of mediation are summarised in Mulcahy with Summerfield (Chapter 2):

1 *The inability of community mediation to reach out to whole communities and heal community rifts*, arising from community mediation's belief that the causes of conflict lie within the community and can be solved by the members of that community.

2 *A lack of success in reducing state control and empowering individuals* – particularly as mediation is supported and funded by the very systems to which it is intended to provide an alternative.

3 *A tendency to reinforce existing inequalities between disputants* – and also that the mediator's rhetoric of equality conceals the ability of the more powerful disputant to coerce an agreement that is more in their favour.

4 *An over-emphasis by the mediators on the value of peace* – mediators encourage compromise and the conflict is too often characterised as a problem of communication or understanding, solvable by a process of mediation that is effectively cathartic or expressive rather than addressing root individual psychological or societal causes.

American academics and practitioners Bush and Folger (1994) have promoted what they define as transformative mediation as an attempt to prevent services providing mediation which reinforces inequalities or which otherwise fails to resolve the underlying issues. By emphasising the empowerment of the parties and their ability to acknowledge concern for each other, a transformative mediation process brings about fundamental and positive change in the parties' relationship which then leads to effective dispute resolution. We are aware of only one neighbour mediation service (Greenwich) that has formally adopted transformative mediation as its mode of practice, but unfortunately the coordinator was unable to commit time to taking part in this review and thus provide us with an assessment of the practical value that transformative mediation offers.

To date this has been an academic debate. Most services are probably unaware that their ethical and value bases are being challenged, and they have therefore been shielded from the need to justify themselves against such criticism. There is opportunity, should the neighbour mediation field wish to take it, for neighbour mediation services to bring their experience and motivation into this debate to refute or at least refine these criticisms against them.

BIBLIOGRAPHY

Bush, R. and Folger, J. (1994) *The Promise of Mediation – Responding to Conflict through Empowerment and Recognition.* Jossey-Bass

Community Legal Service (2001) *Mediation Quality Mark Standard Consultation Paper.* Legal Services Commission

Crowe, S. (1999) *Neighbour Disputes: Responses by Social Landlords.* Chartered Institute of Housing

Dignan, J., Sorsby, A. and Hibbert, J. (1996) *Neighbour Disputes: Comparing the Cost Effectiveness of Mediation and Alternative Approaches.* University of Sheffield, Centre for Criminological and Legal Research

Genn, H. (1999) *Mediation in Action.* Calouste Gulbenkian Foundation

Gowan, S. (ed.) (2000) *Community Safety: Ideas into Action.* Community Links

Gray, J. (2001) *Promotion of Peer Mediation in York Schools.* Safer York Partnership

Hughes, K. and Waddington, G. (2001) *Making Mediation Work for Communities.* Available from the National Assembly of Wales website: www.wales.gov.uk

Hunter, C., Nixon, J. and Shayer, S. (2000) *Neighbour Nuisance, Social Landlords and the Law.* Chartered Institute of Housing for the Joseph Rowntree Foundation

Liebmann, M. (ed.) (1998) *Neighbourhood and Community Mediation.* Cavendish

Liebmann, M. (ed.) (2000) *Mediation in Context.* Jessica Kingsley

Lord Chancellor's Department (1998) *Modernising Justice.* The Stationery Office

McDonough, I. (2001a) *Community Mediation: Choosing a Model of Service Delivery.* SACRO

McDonough, I. (2001b) *Community Mediation: Settling Neighbour Problems Informally.* SACRO

Mediation Works (2001) *A Report on Mediation as a Best Value Approach to Neighbour Nuisance and Anti-social Behaviour in Social Housing.* Mediation Works

Mediation UK (1998) *Practice Standards*. Mediation UK

Mediation UK (2000) *Accreditation Scheme for the Quality Assurance of Mediation Services*. Mediation UK

Mulcahy, L. with Summerfield, L. (2001) *Keeping it in the Community: An Evaluation of the Use of Mediation in Disputes between Neighbours*. The Stationery Office

Note: a comprehensive bibliography on community mediation is provided by Abbey Books (abbeyhall@supanet.com).

APPENDIX: METHODOLOGY

1 Meeting with Mediation UK (Director, and Service Development Coordinator).

2 Analysis of Mediation UK's Service Profiles and the Annual Community Mediation Dispute Survey 2001 (covering the period 1 April 2000 to 31 March 2001).

3 Letter to all neighbour mediation services, informing them about the review, requesting a copy of their latest Annual Report and inviting them to contact Framework if they had a particular desire to be involved further in the review or wanted us to know about specific innovative projects in which they were involved.

4 Telephone interviews with specific services, with questions covering the following:
- What does the service define as community mediation?; what range of mediation services does the service provide?; is mediation always started reactively, or does the service find ways of initiating contact with disputing parties (or working in communities before conflicts emerge)?
- Access to services: what is the take-up of mediation by minority ethnic and 'non-middle-class' service-users? Is there a difference when the mediation process involves children as parties to the dispute?

- Information on use of paid staff and volunteers, including remuneration rates if the service uses paid mediators; management structures.
- Evidence of success: monitoring of standards; which disputes does mediation seem to be particularly effective at addressing?; relevant case studies.
- Has the service considered going for the Quality Mark, or is it already an accredited service?
- Funding: where does the service's funding come from and what opportunities would it seek to take up should more resources permit?